Tempus ORAL HISTORY *Series*

Aberystwyth
voices

Best wishes,

William Troughton

Arthur Lewis, who took many of the photographs in this book, photographed around 1920.

Tempus ORAL HISTORY *Series*

Aberystwyth
voices

Compiled by
William Troughton

TEMPUS

Tempus Publishing Limited
The Mill, Brimscombe Port,
Stroud, Gloucestershire, GL5 2QG

ISBN 0 7524 1892 0

Typesetting and origination by
Tempus Publishing Limited
Printed in Great Britain by
Midway Clark Printing, Wiltshire

Street Party in Lisburne Terrace, 1945.

Contents

Eagle House, Great Darkgate Street now incorporated into Woolworths.

Introduction

Oral history is as old as civilization itself, but it is during the last twenty-five years that oral history has increasingly been recognised as a valuable and unique source of social history. Through the recollections and experiences of people recorded first hand, their childhood, schooldays, work, worship, and pastimes of everyday life unfolds. It is through the medium of a book that these memories can best be shared with a wider audience. It is a relatively recent innovation to publish the spoken word verbatim, capturing both recollections and speech patterns, so it is with this in mind that this book has been compiled as an effort to record everyday life in Aberystwyth during the first half of the twentieth century. It is an exploration of Aberystwyth through personal recollections and experiences. The book does not attempt to tell the life story of those who generously assented to give of their time, but attempts to evoke their world, the Aberystwyth where they grew up, went to school, and later, went to work. As a compiler of this work I have been fortunate to experience these recollections first hand, sometimes spoken with verve and excitement, sometimes with pathos and emotion, often with laughter, but always with enthusiam and fondness. If these last two qualities are lacking and do not translate to the medium of a book, then the fault is mine. Naturally all our memories are prone to occasional failure and there may be some such failings here.

Within the town's boundaries there are people whose unbringing and social class have given them widely differing experiences of the town. It is hoped that this is reflected in the content of the book. Not all of the contributors were born and brought up in Aberystwyth. Some came to Aberyswyth in search of work or because they found love. Others were evacuated here in 1939, carrying gas masks and a few prized possessions under circumstances which by today standards would seem incredulous, even naive and bizarre. The variety of peoples' experiences could amply fill several volumes like this and consequently it has not been possible to include every facet of life within Aberystwyth. Please accept my apologies if you are disappointed to find that a particular aspect of the town, whether the university, the harbour or a particular school or shop does not get the degree of coverage you would have liked.

Should anyone wish to consult the interviews from which this book was compiled, they will find the majority safely stored in the National Library of Wales. Some interviews have been witheld in accordance of the wishes of the interviewees. My grateful thanks is also extended to the National Library of Wales to whom I would like to express my appreciation for permission to use a number of the photographs in this book. Many of these photographs were the work of Arthur Lewis who did so much to record Aberystwyth during the first half of the twentieth century.

Finally I would like to thank most sincerely all those who contributed to the book and whose names are recorded after their respective contributions, also the many friends and colleagues who provided me with a stream of people to interview.

William Troughton
April 2000

One of Glynne Pickford's photos showing the storm damage in January 1938.

Alexandra Road School around 1910. From left to right, top row: Miss Evans (schoolmistress),
C. Smith, L. Humphreys, T. Jones, D. Morgan, W. Burrow, J. Jones, I. Williams, I. Owen,
F. Lewis, T. Beynon, I. Enos, T. Davies, Mr Saer (Headmaster). Centre row: D. Edwards,
A. Jones, W. Edwards, W. Diamond, B. Richards, M. Jenkins, E. Jones, I. Edwards,
W. Edwards, D. Lewis, J. James. Sitting: E. Kay, W. Davies, G. Bearne, G. Minett,
I. Morgan, J. Richards, H. Edwards, T. Lewis, J. Jones, J. Boyce, I. James, J. Evans,
I. Davies, E. Jenkins. In front: S.M. Evans, J. Edwards, M. Richards, -?-, C. Wilson,
D. Morgan, T. Walters.

CHAPTER 1
Childhood

Aberystwyth beach, c. 1930.

A Lively Place

We used to spend the whole day on the beach. All the lovely motor boats were a picture on the water and there'd be shouting, calling people on. Aberystwyth wasn't as poor a place as it is today. It was a lively place. All the shop fronts had to be cleaned and you couldn't shake a mat outside after eight o'clock in the morning on the front, and there wasn't a lorry or a van of any sort in Terrace Road – they weren't allowed to tip their goods after eight o'clock in the morning. There weren't a lot of cars either.

Madge Richards, born 1908

Walking to School

I can remember going all the way to school with a hoop or a top and a whip. We could go all the way over the bridge, down Mill

Terrace Road, c. 1910.

Street to where the roundabout is, there was never any traffic. Where the Salvation Army is, was a lovely place, you could really hit the top there.

Mavis Lowe, born 1924

Clogs

My mother used to put me in clogs in Rheidol Place when I was just walking around for her to know where I was. I suppose I was about two and starting to walk.

Merfyn Jones, born 1919

Our First Car

I think we had our first car sometime around 1923. My mother had a small legacy and she was keen we should have a car. My parents went to the motor show and decided they would have an open, two-seater Sunbeam. It was really a three seater which had been specially made to get three in the front. The agent for Sunbeam was the Gwalia Garage (Jones) at the bottom of North Parade. I remember the night this particular car arrived. My mother went with one of the mechanics from Gwalia Garage, a chap named Prew, up to Wolverhampton to collect it. My father and I walked out past Fronfraith and Nantcaerio at the end of Llanbadarn. We heard the car coming along the flats by Lovesgrove. My mother was driving and she used to like to drive quite rapidly. She saw us and pulled up. It was the first ride I had in a car. It was during holidays from the prep school. It had these three seats in the front and a 'dickie' which could be opened up to give two seats in the back. We had some splendid trips in that, going eventually to the north of Scotland in it. The registration number was EJ 1017. It was a dreadnought grey with black wings and leather upholstery. It had a bench seat which was quite comfortable. I used to sit in the middle.

David Roberts, born 1912

Fascinated by Water

As a child my mother would go and help my grandmother, a widow twice over, at the bottom of High Street – number thirty-three. Her name was Elizabeth Lloyd Thomas. She had to find a copper or two so she took in visitors. My mother used to go down and help her and take a child with her and do the beds, get the meals ready and so forth, that was about 1921. Being aged about five, if that door was open an inch or two I was out of it in a minute. I was attracted to the water. My grandmother, in Welsh, used to say to my mother 'Bydd hwn yn boddi mewn yr ofal yn y mor' (That boy will drown at sea). My mother would go down and look for me but I would be in safe hands with Mr Jenkins who owned one of the biggest boats there. He would pick me up and put me in his boat the *Arrow*. I thought it was marvellous, mind you I was five years of age and everything was big, looking up at the wires and the ropes. The sound of the wind through the rigging was fascinating me, so I always wanted to go to sea. When he wasn't there and I was roaming around, I'd probably fall in the mud. My shoes and my clothes would be dirty. So off I'd go up Penmaesglas Road and standing on the door would be David William's wife and she'd say, 'Ble ti wedi bod nawr 'te ? Dere mewn fan hyn' (Where've you been now ? Come in here.) Then she'd take me down to the cellar where they lived. Down the cellar would be old David Jenkins smoking his pipe by the fireplace, and his parrot that he brought home from sea, on a perch behind him. She would put me on the table and sponge me down. Those were nice people, the people I was brought up with.

Reg White, born 1915

Sunday Evenings

On a summer when I was a girl, there used to be ships coming into the bay. The boatmen would take you out for sixpence. We liked *Pride of the Midlands*. Dad was very friendly with the captain. On a Sunday after going to St Michaels church we'd all go to the pier for an ice cream. Mam and Dad would have a sixpenny, we'd have a threepenny. It was served in a dish with a spoon.

After, we'd go down to the beach, remember we had our best clothes on, and go onto the boat for the last trip home around the pier, Castle Point and into the harbour on *Pride of the Midlands*. We'd get off on the harbour side where there used to be a little ferry run by Teddy James, 'Teddy the Ferry' we used to call him. He had a little rowboat and we'd get in that and be rowed across to Penyrancor and then we just had to walk down the road home.

Mavis Lowe, born 1924

Washing Day

Washing day was always on a Monday and my mother used to do some washing for the others, my grandmother and that. We

Inside the Pier café, c. 1935.

Last trip of the day for Wild Rose, *c. 1935.*

used to have a big boiler, an old Pyre, and we used to boil the clothes in there. You had to put a bit of coal and sticks and sawdust in to keep the fire going. Every Monday, everybody was the same, the clothes were out on the line, white, pure white.

That's how we used to do the Christmas puddings, an all day job. My mother used to make the Christmas puddings and we all had a stir of the mixture, tie 'em up and shove them in the boiler.

Llew Bland, born 1917

Sharks on the Prom

If when they were fishing, the fishermen caught anything unusual in the summer, they used to rig up a tent on the beach in front of the Bay Hotel. The fishermen, I remember them keeping a shark there for weeks, it was stinking, you could hardly go in the tent. I don't remember what they charged, a halfpenny or a penny. I remember as a kid standing outside and collecting the money. You can imagine the sun on a hot day and a tent with this shark lying there. They'd keep it until it was so drewi [smelly] you couldn't go in. Sometimes it was a large crab, anything that was unusual, people used to like to see them.

Merfyn Jones, born 1919

Motorboats

On the promenade there used to be seven motorboats and forty or fifty rowing boats plying their trade, especially when the colliers were here. They'd go out mackerel

fishing before breakfast. Between them they'd have a sovereign. They were getting half a day's wages before breakfast. The boats were *Pride of the Midlands, Worcester Castle, Wild Rose, Kenilworth, Mauretania Birmingham City* and *County of Warwick*. The colliers used to come for a week. Every night there was singing opposite the shelter on the prom by the bandstand. The whole prom was packed with people.

Evan Andrew, born 1916

Mushrooms

When we were living in Llanbadarn I'd get up about six o'clock and go all the way to where the industrial estate is, to the fields there for mushrooms. I'd come home with a big basketful. Lovely mushrooms they were, not like the ones you get in the shops today. They were fresh. There was a field down by Nantcaerio and I remember starting round that field collecting mushrooms with a friend. By the time we got back to where we started there were more, still growing. You could go around again they were growing so quickly. We thought nothing of walking all those miles.

Doris Price

Money for the Pictures

The coaches, four-in-hand used to go up Penparcau hill and we all used to go and sing behind them and they used to throw money out. We'd get money like that to go to the pictures.

Watty Chamberlain, born 1906

Mrs Doris Price and Mrs Collison.

Elysian Grove

Elysian Grove was beautiful when we were young. It was lit up in the summer with fairy lights. Couples used to go for walks right up past the golf links, that way onto the top of Consti. We children, the best part for us was all the amusements, all sorts of things, see-saws, swings, everything you could think of. There were pierrots, high class pierrots. We didn't go often because we weren't allowed. There were competitions for children and young boys. One was to sing while holding a piglet. The thing would fall out of their arms, then they wouldn't win. If they could keep hold of the piglet until the end of the song they could keep it. One of my brothers won it and took it home to my mother. At that time we lived in North Road. My mother wouldn't keep it what with children in the house. She gave it to the milkman or the butcher or someone.

Madge Richards, born 1908

Sunday School Trip

The big day was the Sunday school trip which would be Whit Tuesday. It was the only time we would ever go on a train. I remember we went to Shrewsbury once. My mother went with my cousin who was years older than I. She said 'Get on that train, you behave yourself and make sure that you catch that train to come back'. We got back safe and sound. After a short while there was a policeman at the door 'Is there a Mrs Andrew live here ?' My father said yes. 'Just

Elysian Grove, c. 1910.

Harry Collins' Merry Mascot Minstrels, regular performers in Elysian Grove.

15

to let you know she's missed the train and will be coming in on the mail.' She didn't hear the end of that for years.

Evan Andrew, born 1916

Working on the Boats

I mitched school for two months when I was thirteen to work on the boats. You were doing something you loved to do. With the visitors you'd be baiting the hooks for them and you'd take the fish off the hooks. With a mackerel flipping about in the boat the visitors would be screaming. It wasn't like today with feathers. It was a single hook with a weight. You might get a box of mackerel depending on how they were running. You'd come back and gill them with bits of twine – put the twine through the gill and the mouth. Everybody got a turn at fishing so you'd be trailing five lines. You weren't allowed to carry more than thirty-two passengers. Most of these people would be in digs for a week or a fortnight. At the end of the trip the boatmen would offer them the fish. Some would have four, some six, some a dozen. You'd go out at ten o' clock and come in at half past twelve. Maybe there'd be a few dozen mackerel left, so as a kid I'd take a box up to the top of the slip, put it on the tilt and sell them thirteen for a shilling. On the other side would be Gwilym Williams doing the same thing for his father.

Roger James, born 1926

Roast Potatoes

Cacen Lloyd used to sell groceries, cooked meat, ham, all that kind of thing. There were tearooms and a bakehouse at the back. After the bread was done, at night they used to do roast potatoes in the ovens, six a penny. They had a maid called Lizzie. As kids we used to go into the bakehouse and say 'Lizzie, Mrs Lloyd is calling.' In she'd go and by the time she came back our pockets were full of potatoes.

Evan Andrew, born 1916

Fresh Bread

Mrs Lloyd kept a bakehouse in South Road where we used to take our bread to be baked. Just before you come to where the garage in South Road was, there's a place with steps going down where you could get out by the river. In the house there were steps going down to the cellar. Down in the cellar was an oven. Mr Lloyd had a farm, Gogerddan way somewhere, and you got wood from there. When the wood in the oven was burning with a blue flame they used to take it out and put the bread in. The bread used to be lovely. As children we used to carry it over the bridge and be eating the crusts on the way home. The flavour of it was delicious. It closed down about 1914. Then we were taking bread to Chamberlain, my uncle who run the bakehouse in Bridge Street. Everybody made their own bread in their own tins. They used put a certain mark on top to know them. There was a glorious flavour to it.

Watty Chamberlain, born 1906

Twopence or a Teacake

James, on upper Great Darkgate Street was a baker. He had two sisters, round little fat ladies. Farmers used to bring wood in on open carts. We'd run then to help them carry it in through the back. We'd get twopence or a teacake. Being kids we were always hungry, so we had the teacake.

Evan Andrew, born 1916

Cawl

We used to have an old fashioned fire place, like a whole hob and the old cawl (soup) would be going there for a couple of days. My mother would add extra vegetables to it.

Llew Bland, born 1917

Lobsters

There was one boy, same age as myself, Donny James, he knew every hole between the pier rocks and Castle Point. In those days you could guarantee he'd go on there and come back with four or five, two or three pound lobsters. You couldn't give the crabs away.

Roger James, born 1926

Smoking

You know Mill Street, there used to be a little sweet shop half way along on the right at the bottom of George Street, it's a ladies hairdresser now. That shop was owned by Billy Bon-bon's family. He used to get Ardour cigarettes from the family and a gang of us used to go down the band room down Park Avenue. We used to go behind there and smoke cigarettes. We

were about eleven years of age. By that time we were used to smoking regularly. Remember, this was the time of the great days of the cinema, pictures we used to call it, and of course all the stars were always smoking and there was a big palaver to light your cigarette. As kids we were always aping this, smoking cigarettes-you were a man! By the mid-teens it was well engrained. It was difficult to get enough money for cigarettes. Players Weights were five for twopence. Then in the railway station there was a machine where you could buy two cigarettes for a penny, 'Two in One' or something.

Edward Ellis, born 1922

Swimming Baths

The old swimming baths were supposed to be six foot at the deep end but I could stand up in it. It was six foot to the top of the bath, not to the top of the water. It was sea water which was pumped in. For the first few days it was delightful. After the water had been in over a week you could practically stand on it. You couldn't see the bottom of the bath. I can remember on one occasion a gentleman diving in and coming up with his nose split. There was only about two foot six inches of water where he dived in. I saw another gentleman come in, now we had a diving board about six foot, this gentleman who was well over six foot dived in and his legs never went under the water. The water was only about five foot three inches in the deepest end. When he came up his front teeth were missing.

John Lewis, born 1913

You Had to Speak English Didn't You?

We were Welsh. My parents never spoke English. Of course times changed and the older members [of the family] married Englishmen, one married an Irishman. English came into the home. You had to speak English didn't you?

Madge Richards, born 1908

Evans Chips

We used to go to Evans Chips in Bridge Street. On a Friday my mother would give us twopence each and my friend and I would go for a twopenny plate. We'd go in the back room and Mr Evans would come and serve us with a fork and plate. We'd have a fishcake and chips. The Italians had most of the chip shops but we always went to that one.

Mavis Lowe, born 1924

Cordrays

You know where the craft shop is in Northgate Street, that used to be a chip shop called Cordrays. As a kid I remember going down there with a basin for the chips. You'd take a basin with you and a small jug for peas. You'd put a piece of paper round the basin and off you'd go home.

Edward Ellis, born 1922

Shoes

You could buy screws and nails from Robert's timber yard. Then you'd go down to the tanyard opposite the slaughterhouse. My brother was working there as a fellmonger. People used to buy leather and tap their own boots. Nearly everybody had a last. In the summer when you were children you never wore shoes. You were always running about without them and in the rivers swimming. Good old times they were.

Watty Chamberlain, born 1906

Hanging on to the Fender

I used to go down to the harbour with my father as a kiddie. I only remember little bits because I was only four years of age. It was blowing and in those days if it was blowing you'd go down and put extra ropes out on the boats, especially if they were big tides. On this particular day I'd gone down with my father and I fell. The boat was moored alongside the steps where the crane was with another boat on the outside of us. There were fenders on the boat to keep it off the wall. My father had gone into the cabin for something. Why I stepped off the deck I don't know but I fell in the water between the boat and the quay. I shouted 'Dad, Dad'. Fortunately he heard me and pulled me out. We had fenders on the boat and I was hanging on to that.

Des Davies, born 1926

Dickie

I remember a German ship *Dickie* coming in. My father used to take me aboard and I used to have bread and jam and things. That ship could just turn between the main wharf and the St Davids wharf. She was touching both sides when she turned and you could step on at either end.

Merfyn Jones, born 1919

Clareen

The ships I remember in my time were two fore and aft sailing ships, the *Clareen* and the *Rockingham*. Most of the townspeople know about the *Clareen* because she hit the rocks at the end of the stone jetty and made a hole in the bottom. They managed to get it to the quay wall before it sunk. They discharged the cargo of coal and the *Clareen* was put at the top of the harbour near the gap. For years us kids played on it. Eventually it was sold for one pound to a Mr Jack Bennison. It was towed across the harbour and beached there and eventually they went there with their saws and such and she was cut up. They tell me that a lot of the wood was made into staircases and doorways in Caradoc Road and Queens Road because it was pitch pine.

Reg White, born 1915

The FA Cup

In 1927, Cardiff City were playing in the cup final. Dick Wright who lived opposite, he

Clareen *became an unofficial playground before being broken up.*

and his brother-in-law made a wireless set. They were the only ones who had a wireless set. Cardiff were playing the Arsenal. The room where the set was on the table was packed, everybody was shoulder to shoulder in the room. Half way up the street and half way down the street was packed. Cardiff won and it's the only time the FA Cup has come out of England.

Evan Andrew, born 1916

Model Boats

The old paddling pool has gone of course. My father, Arthur Lewis, had this training in engineering. He'd make model boats and put an engine in them. My brother and I would stand at the end of the paddling pool and send the boats back.

There were narrow strips of thick wood you could walk on. Over the years the council never bothered to repair it. A bit further on you'd go on the rocks. We used to catch some lovely bass off the end of Castle Point. I used to go fishing with my brother and catch devillers just below where Cor Y Castell was. They were very difficult to catch.

Gwladys Ednyfed Thomas

The Paddling Pool

The paddling pool by Castle Point was going then. I remember falling in there. We used to go there because it was clean water. It only used to be full when the tide was in.

Mavis Lowe, born 1924

Cocoa Tins

I remember Arthur Lewis at the Mart getting Cadburys Cocoa tins and opening them up along the seams to get a flat piece of tin. He'd bend them around a model of a hull, like a template, and solder them together. Then he'd put in an engine that ran on methylated spirits. He made some beautiful boats.

Des Davies, born 1926

Lantern-Slide Shows

The lantern slides my father chose, I think he must have done them from photographs. When he used to get them ready he used to put passe-partout [black tape] around the edges and I used to help him on a winters evening. He used to go around with these slides when he was asked to show them. There was one of John Bull tempting a dog with a string of sausages and another of a clown skipping. These were for the interval. Another one was of a sailing ship with the words, 'To those in Peril on the Sea'. Once, in the hall at Trefechan, this was showing and I turned around and there were all these women crying. I couldn't make out why they were crying. My mother said it was because they had lost somebody at sea. I was very subdued then.

Gwladys Ednyfed Thomas

Market Day

Monday was market day. Farmers used to come into town on their carts and park along the back of the market hall. They used to bring piglets in the carts and put a net over the cart

Local children enjoying the paddling pool, c. 1930.

to stop the piglets escaping. They used to back the carts up against the market and take the horses out of the shafts. We used to get a penny for holding the horses heads while they were being taken out of the shafts. We used to go with them then to the stables at the back of the Farmers Arms and the Angel Inn. About four o'clock in the afternoon when the market was finishing we'd go down and bring the horses back up. There was always hay for the horses and troughs. We used to play there as kids when there weren't any horses there.

Des Davies, born 1926

The Pig Market

I remember the pig market every Monday around the old market hall. People would come and barter with the farmers for them, it wasn't an auction. They used to come to father's warehouse for a tea chest. My father always charged the farmer threepence because having got a tea-chest to take the piglets home in, they would then want to borrow a hammer and nails and then borrow string to tie around the tea chest. Then they wanted to borrow a truck. Invariably they would borrow a truck to take the piglets to the local bus and never bring the truck back.

John Lewis, born 1913

The Mart

On a Monday you'd have the sheep and cattle coming into town all on the road, drovers would be bringing them, driving them over the bridge, into Smithfield and down to the slaughterhouse.

Mavis Lowe, born 1924

The Lewis family outside their home in High Street, c. 1930. Mrs Gwladys Ednyfed Thomas is the elder of the two girls.

Plague of Rats

I remember the plague of rats in the old market hall and the stables around. They used to come into my father's warehouse and eat their way through, particularly into any confectionery that contained nuts. They could empty a box practically. Eventually they employed people to catch these rats. They used to go into the market with ferrets and terriers. I can recall being allowed into the market to see this taking place. On one occasion a rat came out and I hit out at it with my foot and hit the terrier. I was excluded from then on. In my time you could see the rats going up and down the gutters and so on. They had to put tin barriers around the stalls to stop the rats climbing up the stalls and going along to get at the chickens. That happened for a couple of years and suddenly they just disappeared, migrated.

John Lewis, born 1913

Christmas

At Christmas we always had a goose. We'd have it for ten shillings. We used to go to George Street. There used to be two sisters who lived there, from a family who had a farm in Llanddeiniol. Deiniol the

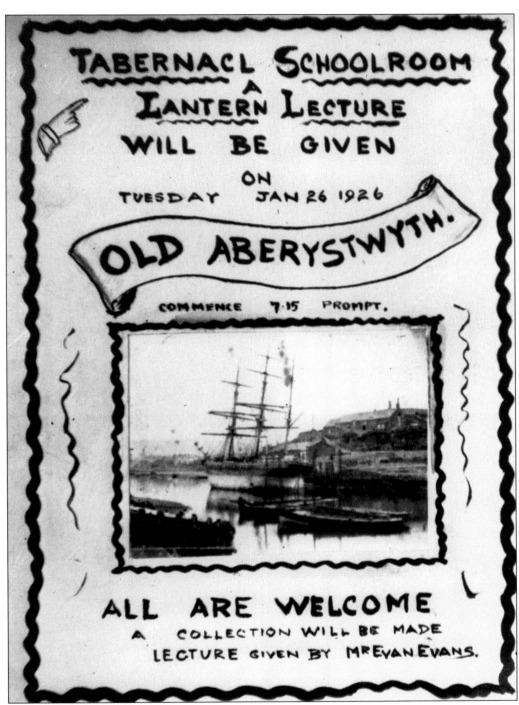

An advertisement for one of Arthur Lewis' lantern slide shows.

house in George Street was called. The one sister lived on the farm. Every Christmas she used to bring her poultry to the house to be displayed. We used to go there, mam and I, on Christmas Eve afternoon into the parlour and all the geese were there on a table with a beautiful white tablecloth. All geese, no turkeys then. Mam used to save all year to get a goose.

Christmas was lovely. Trimmings on everything, balloons everywhere. Dad would get the ladder out and be helping us. Always a lovely big tree. Times were hard but we always had presents from mam and dad. Dolls I liked. My sister never bothered with dolls. A handbag she liked and she'd stuff everything into it. Train sets Ray would have. There'd be a tree at the top of Great Darkgate Street by the town clock.

Mavis Lowe, born 1924

The Parlour

Christmas time we were always in the front room. Presents were very few – an apple, orange and a few nuts, maybe one small present and that was it. Tea was in the parlour. That was the only time we saw the parlour. At Christmas time in the market hall there were tables right along the centre. The farmers then would bring their geese, turkeys and chickens and the place would be full.

Evan Andrew, born 1916

Calennig (New Year's gift)

Before New Years Day we would have been busy sewing little bags to put our Calennig in. We did it and yet there was nothing in it. It was begging really. Lots of our neighbours would say 'Cofiwch

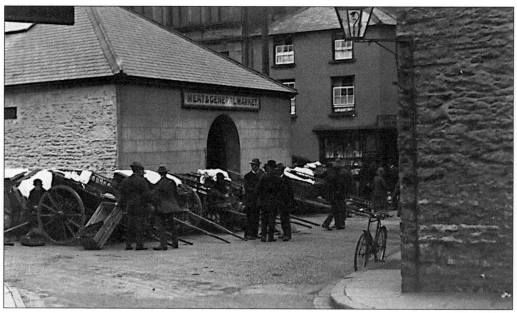

Carts at the back of the market hall, c. 1930.

galw' (remember to come), and we would go. There was a little old lady, Mrs Jones, lived in High Street always – short, very, very rosy cheeks. New Years Day we'd knock on the door and there she'd be with a new penny. New Years Eve there would be a prayer meeting in Tanycae Sunday school and there'd be some people there giving us pennies. But on New Years Day we'd go to Evans, the paper shop on the corner near where Queen Street goes up [Hot Bread Shop today]. We all used to go to him and he'd be giving out sweets, comics, transfers and all kinds of things. He was very kind.

Gwladys Ednyfed Thomas

New Years Day

We used to go to the brewery every New Year and they used to throw pennies for the kids. When I was a child, they'd go to the bank for new pennies, and Mr Henry and Dr David Roberts would throw the pennies out. They used to do that to see us scrambling for them. After that we'd all line up in the yard and get a penny again as you went out through the gate. They kept that up for years.

We used to knock on peoples' doors and say 'Blwyddyn Newydd Dda' or 'Happy New Year' and hold your cap out. In the country they used to sing for it. We'd go round town and all, nobody would turn you away, they always gave you something. In shops you'd get an apple or an orange or something. You used to do a bit of money on that day. You don't see nobody doing it now; everybody collected Calennig in those days, girls and boys. You were up early that morning and out quick. You had to finish at twelve o'clock. You didn't get nothing after twelve.

Watty Chamberlain, born 1906

CHAPTER 2

Schooldays

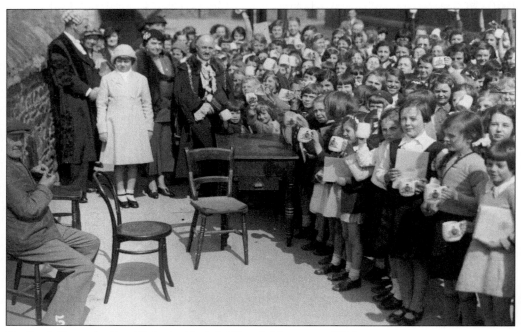

Pupils of Alexandra Road School with their Silver Jubilee mugs, 1935.

Fast Asleep

I had two brothers. My older brother went to church school and my other brother, who was only a year younger than him, cried because he wanted to go to school. Of course my mother couldn't take him to school. In those days little boys wore skirts, they didn't wear trousers. One day the teacher said to my mother, make a little skirt for him and he can come to school. He was delighted to go to school. My mother went to fetch him home after his first day at school and there he was with his head on the desk, fast asleep

Madge Richards, born 1908

Miss Marles Thomas

I started off on the South Terrace in Miss Marles Thomas's pre-prep school. There were

North Road School, c. 1910.

one or two other local people who sent their children there. It was a very stormy and awkward place to get to, always pouring with rain or frightfully windy. The first floor room, which Miss Marles Thomas had, was a very nice room which looked out towards the sea. Eventually she retired and built herself a house in Devils Bridge. I was about eight when I went away to school and must have been at Miss Marles Thomas for two or three years. I would be taken by the nurse over the bridge and along South Road. Then I went away to Wellington in Shropshire, which was a very good prep school. After prep school I went to Shrewsbury where my grandparents lived.

David Roberts, born 1912

A Right Tartar

There was a big wall between the girls' school and the boys' school. Miss Davies was the headmistress of the girls' school. She was a right tartar. She married a vicar from Devils Bridge and was a Mrs Wynne after. The infants was in the front. I can remember my teachers there – Miss Lewis, Miss Tibbot and Miss Samuel, who was the headmistress.

Evan Andrew, born 1916

All Large Classes

We went to the board school, it became the Alexandra Road school afterwards. We had a wonderful headmistress. She was very, very strict. Looking back she was excellent. She could knock anything into anyone. You didn't dare not learn with her. She had a way with her. She used to peep over the partitions. They talk about schools having classes that are too large, and all this nonsense. I was never in a small class, they were all large classes. Some of them were different ages in the classroom. One teacher had to cope with the lot and you had to behave. There was no nonsense in those days. They had a pointer and you only had to see the pointer and you behaved.

Madge Richards, born 1908

Alexandra Road School

The boys were one side and we were the other side. They'd be kicking the ball over the wall and we'd be keeping it and then there'd be a row and we'd have to throw it back. The boys would climb up the wall and be shouting things at the girls. The toilets were right down the bottom end of the yard. It was one long building with cubicles. The seats were wooden. Every now and then they'd be flushed from one end right through. You had to get out quick or you'd be soaking wet.

Cookery class we had with Miss Jones Morolwg. She used to live on the Buarth. We had to wear a coarse apron. Perhaps we'd be scrubbing the porch one day, then cooking the next, then housewifery. We always came home for dinners. There used to be school dinners, twopence they used to be. They were served opposite Somerield, in a building that Avery Scales took on after. It went right through like a big shed. Proper workhouse it used to be with long tables all the way down.

Mavis Lowe, born 1924

Miss Trotter

I missed a lot of school. I was very bronchial and asthmatic as a kid. They sent me to a private school because I was missing so much, Miss Trotters, a preparatory school in North Road. I stayed there until I came away, I didn't go to Ardwyn. It was only about twenty-five kids. She was very good and had a good staff. I

Arthur House football team, Alexandra Road School, 1936-1937. From left to right, back row: Mr Davies (Headmaster), Islwyn Fisher-Davies, Tecwyn Evans, Alwyn Williams, Trevor Hopton, Gwilym Williams, Gary Lewis, Gerald Thomas, Des Davies. Front row: Eustace Davies, Caradoc Davies, Donald James, Albert Davies, Wyndham Owen, Mr Jones (teacher).

wasn't very good at anything. I was top at art, drawing that sort of thing, I was top of the school in that. I was more keen on going into the family business. I did have an exam, Cambridge I think it was. I managed to scrape through.

Glynne Pickford, born 1909

Jailbirds Arise

Our football field when we were kids used to be next to the old refectory by the castle. One wall was Fossett Robert's wall. Sometimes somebody would report us to the police. You'd have one policeman coming up through the churchyard, one coming up Laura Place. Once we got caught! The case was on a Wednesday in the town hall. Mr Saer went in to the class on the day and said 'Jailbirds arise.' It was nearly the whole class! We were fined five shillings for playing football on the street.

Evan Andrew, born 1916

Give Him a Clipsen

My father and mother always used to speak Welsh. My grandmother came originally from Goginan and then lived in Llanbadarn for years and years. When we were kids we used to come home from school and our mother would talk to us in Welsh, and we'd answer in English. There'd be a row then and my grandmother would say, 'Give him a clipsen' (a clout). We didn't have much Welsh in school, just half an hour a week or so, and it was more like a lazy half-hour kind of thing. You didn't learn nothing. They used to speak all Welsh in the house, but we didn't, we used

to answer in English. We understood what they were talking about so we always used to get into a row about that.

Llew Bland, born 1917

Board School

I was in the board school by the station. It was the board school when I was there but it was the Welsh School when my daughter went there. I enjoyed my schooldays. There were quite a lot in the classes. I started with Miss Lewis in the infants, then Miss Chamberlain and Miss James. I went from there to Ardwyn. I didn't do the matric. I was there for four years then left school to go to work in Pickfords the photographers.

Florrie Bevan, born 1916

Sitting By a Girl

In a way I enjoyed school, but the teachers used to be strict. I remember going to Mr Saer's funeral. He was the headmaster, and he died, and we all had to go to his funeral, the whole school. If you were naughty you were put to sit by a girl. I had to sit by a girl many a time, for not doing homework properly, talking that sort of thing.

Llew Bland, born 1917

Alexandra Road School

Miss Tibbott was my first teacher in infants, then Miss Saer the previous headmaster's daughter taught me. Mr Davies was headmaster. There were about twenty-eight to thirty in my class. I think classes were always about that size when I was in school. After the infants we went on to the boys school next door and started in standard one, then standard two and all that. When you got to standard five you could sit the scholarship and went from there to Ardwyn. The scholarship class was taught by Mr Evans. If you didn't go to Ardwyn you went to standards six and seven and left school at fourteen.

Des Davies, born 1926

Speaking Welsh

It was nearly all Welsh in Aber then. I should speak Welsh, but I don't. That was all my parents spoke. My grandfather came from Kidderminster and he learned to speak Welsh. I understand Welsh but never tried to speak it because I went to Alexandra Road School and not much Welsh was allowed. You didn't get a row for speaking Welsh, but they didn't bring Welsh on. You may get a bit of poetry, but you weren't learning Welsh. Evans Llanilar was our teacher and Saer was the headmaster. All the Trefechan boys were a bit rough-house.

Watty Chamberlain, born 1906

Armistice Day

On Armistice Day they used to do sketches on the stage in the Coliseum and re-enact the trenches. It was very dramatic. It quite changed our outlook. I think we had a day off for Armistice. I used to be in the Brownies. We all followed each other from the town hall to Terrace Road, Great

Darkgate Street, and right round to the war memorial. Armistice Day was always on the 11th of November. The Red Cross, the Girl Guides, all the people you can think of were there. I remember with the Brownies being in a little brown cotton dress, though I think I had something warmer underneath, and a round straw hat. There was a service at the war memorial. It was cold though. It was the done thing for everybody to turn out. Aberystwyth was always very keen on bands.

Gwladys Ednyfed Thomas

Medals

We used to have medals in school for attendance, lead things they were. I got one for attending school for three years without a break.

Llew Bland, born 1917

Gilbert & Sullivan

I was in two of the operatic productions at Ardwyn. The first one they performed was *HMS Pinafore* and us senior boys, well it was beneath our dignity to take part in it and so on. But they had a wonderful soiree after, and the next year I took part. I had no voice. I did *Iolanthe and the Gondoliers*.

John Lewis, born 1913

School Concerts

We used to use the Parish Hall. I can't remember which one it was, but I had to

Some of the cast of Iolanthe performed by pupils of Ardwyn Grammar School, 1940.

march around with a sword. I always remember looking up and someone had stuck a potato on the end of it.

Noel Butler, born 1913

Like Poison

My least favourite teachers were Miss Dalley and Miss Forster. If Miss Forster was teaching today, she would have been kicked out for the way she talked to the children. We were mentally deficient and imbeciles.

My parents sent me, wrongly, to Ardwyn a year before I should have gone. Miss Forster was my form mistress and I can see her now. She would come into the form room and give a twirl and her gown would blow out behind her as she floated onto the dais. I hadn't got a friend in the school, as I had gone a year younger than I should have done. Her opening remarks were not, 'Good morning children' but 'Lewis stand up'. Little Lewis stood up and she asked, 'Are you a brother to those awful twins that have just left?' With hindsight I'd have said no of course. We went into the main hall for prayers. Miss Dalley used to take prayers until the headmaster came in. I put my satchel on the floor and the boy in front trod on it and I said, 'You're standing on my satchel.' With that the deputy headmistress [said] 'That boy there', and my form-mistress floated across the stage and whispered across the stage, 'brother to the twins!' I got a one hour detention. I had hardly been in school ten minutes. I hated those two like poison. But the men, they were great. Sam Mitchell, he used to take games and so on. He had a terrific sense of humour, a fine chap. Tom James was very good. David Jenkins married my wife's best friend. W.D. Lewis was the art master. He was a member of Salem. He wasn't a brilliant art master and

31

Interior of National School, North Road in 1925, now demolished.

Ardwyn Grammar School as seen from the drive of the National Library of Wales, c.1930.

used to take woodwork as well. Twm Salmon was a nice chap, but no teacher. He used to write five problems on the board and just change the figures as he changed lessons.

John Lewis, born 1913

Dread

I didn't appreciate Ardwyn as much as I should have done. Dafws Latin, Mrs Davies Latin was my form mistress. She lived in a house at the top of Plascrug, where the substation is now. There was a nice house there and she lived in it. It was pulled down in the war years probably. I remember her living there because I used to dread passing there. Lalla Thomas was the English teacher, Chris Jones – Physics, Johnny Chlorine – Chem, Sam Mitch, Old Stimson – PE.

Merfyn Jones, born 1919

Thirteen Detentions

School days were the happiest days of my life, I enjoyed myself there. We had detention of course. One term I had thirteen detentions on my report.

John Lewis, born 1913

School Dinners

D.C. Lewis started school dinners in Ardwyn. They were sixpence a dinner, two shillings a week if you stayed for the week. They were absolutely cracking dinners.

Mrs Burns was the cook. She was a dear old soul. When I was a prefect I was on permanent dinner duty. We ate the dinners in the central hall. D.C. Lewis built on a kitchen. If you look towards the geography department the kitchen was at that end of the central hall. On the left hand side was a door going into it. It was built between the girls' playground and the boys' playground. Dan the cleaner was very officious. One of Dan's jobs was wheeling the dinners out on the tea trolley. He was very careful about counting and making sure nobody got two dinners. I remember on one occasion he came out and he

T. Ainsleigh Jones, highly regarded headmaster of the National School from 1892-1925 and a keen actor.

33

Ardwyn Chess Club, 1931.

John Lewis as Luiz in the Ardwyn production of the Gondoliers, 1931.

passed the plates of rice pudding down. This lad got the plate of rice pudding and put it under the table and held it there with his knee. Dan was there miscounting and trying to check up and Dan was always spot on. What happened was the pudding was red hot and it ended up on the floor, much to Dan's delight as his count was right.

John Lewis, born 1913

An Active Lad

I had the record ten seconds for one hundred yards; the only one who'd done it before was Jack London a big, beefy negro who was in Ardwyn before my time. I had colours in gym. I was quite an active lad.

Noel Butler, born 1913

Pupils of Ardwyn giving a gymnastic display at the Royal Welsh Show, Aberystwyth, 1933.

Ardwyn Cricket Team, c.1936.

Ardwyn Grammar School Tennis team, 1936-1937.

Prefects at Ardwyn Grammar school, c. 1937.

Games

For games the form captain had to go to the headmaster and ask. There was no regular games. It all depended on goodwill. We would have first period in the afternoon, then go down through the cemetery to what is now the Aber town rugger field. Well, of course it was below the river level and it was a quagmire. There was no groundsman and there was a stench from the mud. There were two semi-circular tin sheds, one for the boys and one for the girls. They were never locked and overnight, gentlemen of the road used to sleep in them. You can imagine what condition they were in. If it rained, one section of the field would be covered in water. There were no showers, baths or anything. You played and came home covered in mud. It was grim. When I was in the football team, come the football season the grass would have grown so they used to get a farmer to come and cut the grass. One year when I was captain, we couldn't get a farmer and we borrowed a machine and got a farmer's son from school to come and cut the grass before the game. There was no training, if you happened to be good at the game it was because of your own good fortune and ability. Then we had to put the goalposts up. The stench from the mud was unbearable. When we played inter school matches we changed in the school. We were very discourteous really because we had to go through the cemetery down to the field, and as soon as the final whistle would blow we were off like mad to get up to the kitchen to get a bowl of hot water. Then we used to change in that little cloakroom near to the men's staffroom. Imagine eleven kids trying to change in there. The washbowls were tiny little washbowls and we used to have a tin of hot water from the kitchen. I don't know what the visiting teams did as I never saw them getting hot water. We'd have tea for the visiting side in the old kitchen, on the left-hand side above the old shelters. Some of the girls would make tea for the visitors.

John Lewis

Welsh

My father insisted we learn Welsh. Trouble was my parents came from north Wales and they had a different vocabulary to the south-Walians. This man was a south Walian. We used to go to school and we weren't using the words he was using at all. We weren't very bright at all I can tell you.

Madge Richards, born 1908

CHAPTER 3

The World of Work

Mrs Violet Davies at work behind the counter of the family business at twenty-six Pier Street.

Teviotdales

I started working at fourteen. You were straight out of school and into a job. I went to Teviotdales for three or four years, getting ten shillings a week. Teviotdales was a cake shop on the bottom, a cafe upstairs, and a bakehouse behind that came out on Cambrian Street. They had a big warehouse the other side of Cambrian Street. In Teviotdales was Miss Burns, a direct descendant of Thomas Burns. In charge of

the cafe was Miss Evans. Bateman, Caradoc Jones from Llanbadarn, Dai Pritchard, Tom Gerry, me and Idwal Hicks worked there. There were four who worked there at night and six or seven in the day. There was a horse and truck going round the town selling bread, with the big shop selling cakes and things. They were doing well. They didn't waste nothing, we even used to sieve the coke after the fires.

I had the sack for hitting Dai Pritchard from Corris. He was working with me. I said something and he told me, 'Speak English for Christsakes.' I said, 'When you come here first you couldn't speak a word of English.' Then he hit me so I hit him and had the sack for it. I got a job in my uncle's bakehouse, then came into the brewery.

Watty Chamberlain, born 1906

S.N. Cooke

I hated Ardwyn. I got out as soon as I could and got a job with S.N. Cooke in Pier Street as an apprentice to Miss Pearce. To even get into S.N. Cooke was an accomplishment. S.N. Cooke was a very stylish shop where Stewarts Seconds is now. It sold clothes and linen and woollens, good quality goods. I was there about nine years. The shop was on one floor, all open, but everyone had their own department to look after. I was in charge of the wool department. Two brothers owned the company. They had shops in Birmingham and Shrewsbury and were well known in Birmingham. They were bombed during the war and moved down here. The two brothers were well to do and used to come to the shop in a big car with a chauffeur. There were five always working in the shop, and then for the summer sales, it went up to about fifteen. They used to bring girls from their Birmingham store down all through the summer for the sales. It was such a big sale the bosses used to live on top of the shop.

All your wages were made up of commission. You had to make so many pounds in the week before you got commission. Without commission you only got about twelve shillings a week. That was just about enough to pay for your frocks. It wasn't overalls then, it was frocks. It was that sort of shop. Twelve shillings was basic and

you had to pay for your dress out of that every week. You'd take home more than a pound a week.

Kwik Save went there after it closed. They ripped all the inside out, it was all mahogany fitments, beautiful.

Phyllis Morgan

Peacocks

I left school at fourteen, you had to leave at fourteen then, and went to work in Peacocks. It was after the fire so it is where it is now. I was there four years and the war came. Peacocks were happy times. I was on the baby counter. The manager was as good as gold. I used to deal with all the people who were having babies. Then I went on the mens' counter. Shirts were one shilling elevenpence and two shillings elevenpence. Trousers were two shillings elevenpence. On the first Monday of the fair, cyflogi, we would be working until eight at night. All the farmers would be coming in and buying shirts, trousers and underwear, socks everything. The three Mondays of the fair

A 1930s advertisement for S.N. Cooke.

Terrace Road. Peacocks moved to their present site shortly after their previous premises were destroyed by the fire at the Palladium Cinema in 1935.

we'd be busy. We'd stay open late on those Mondays. Usually it was nine o'clock until half past five.

Mavis Lowe

How I Went to Sea

I'm fascinated by water and you can't keep me away from it. I used to help Mr Baden Davies down the harbour. A man used to come down to talk to him when he was home, a sailor who had been at sea fifty years or more. His name was Mr John Johnson. We called him Jack. Jack Johnson lived in High Street and he named the house Stella. It's half way up High Street on the right hand side when you go up towards the Ship and Castle. Jack had been at sea all his life. He was a Mancunian but I thought he was from

Aberystwyth. After sailing with him on many ships during the war, I was surprised to find out that he came from Manchester. That was why I could get no Welsh out of him, though my Welsh is limited. Baden would say to Mr Johnson, if you ever want a boy, take this one with you. As it was, when he next come home three or six months later, he said to me, 'Do you want to go to sea son?' I said, 'Yes sir.' 'Well, tell your mother you're coming with me tonight.' My little heart was ticking over now, here I go, I'm going to sea. I went home and said, 'Mam I'm going to sea tonight with Mr Johnson.'

The thing then was to raise the money for the fare to go with Mr Johnson. Things were thrown in the suitcase. You had to take everything with you. You had to take a pillow with you. You had to take a sheet with you. If you were posh a counterpane and a blanket, they didn't supply bedding. I put my clothes in, my toothbrush, a pair of shoes and various things a boy wants to go to sea with. We got on the mail at six o'clock at night and travelled up to Glasgow. We got to Glasgow in the early hours of the morning and found out what time the trains were going to what they call the tail of the bank. We were going to Greenock. When we got to Greenock we got a taxi to the gangway at the bottom of the ship. The ship was the *Stan Grant*. It was one of the Clan liners, Scottish. It was called the *Stan Grant* because it was the Stanhope Shipping Company. About thirty-five to forty feet up, was a ship's officer leaning over the rail in white flannels, a white shirt and a peaked cap with the company badge on the front, and he knew Mr Johnson because Johnson was the bosun. The bosun on a ship was the foreman of the sailors. He said, 'Is that you Johnson? Come aboard'. Up we went and the ship's officer said, 'Who's that lad down below?' 'That's the ordinary seaman sir, White'; 'Oh no you're supposed to bring an ordinary seaman called Davies, not White.'

Apparently the bosun, Johnson, had a telegram to tell him to join the ship at so and so hours, on Monday 13th so and so and bring ordinary seaman. But it didn't say no name so Johnson thought he'd take me as an ordinary seaman. I was a misprint, I shouldn't be there. Here's a boy standing on the quay in Greenock, hundreds of miles from home. They had a chat on deck and I was told to come up and I went up on deck. The chief officer said to me 'What's your name son?' 'Reginald White, sir.' 'Right, go with Johnson'. I went with Johnson and we found his room with a brass plate outside saying Bosun's Room. It contained a six foot bunk, a settee and a table to do your writing on. I was to sleep on the settee because the ship was getting overhauled and repaired. A terrible noise went on there with riveting and cutting ironwork up and all this. Day and night it was going, twenty-four hours a day. There wasn't much sleep with it but you got up at half past five and you had to turn to by six o'clock and you worked until five o'clock at night. So I slept on the settee and Johnson slept on his bunk. We needed our sleep as we'd travelled up the night before. In the middle of the night something fell on top of me. I thought it was

The Stan Grant, *Reg White's first ship*.

either a kitten or a cat and I woke up with a start and I shouted 'Jack' and he woke up with a start. 'A cat or something has fallen on top of me.' 'Put the light on,' he said. How did I know where the light was? I put the light on and it was a rat. On top of the deckhead there was a ventilator and it must have crawled up the ventilator and fell down on top of me. There were two of us running back and fore trying to get the rat out. It was comical.

Reg White, born 1915

Working at twelve

I started work when I was twelve years old for Evan Jenkins, the grocer in Princess Street. In the morning I'd go to the shop before school, off to school at nine, go home midday, have a pot of broth, then in the shop after school. Saturday was a full day. I'd go up the Buarth with my little book, remember I was only twelve, Sea View Place and High Street taking the orders. I'd take them back to the shop, make them all up and deliver them with a little hand-truck. I'd be working until eleven o'clock at night. All the shops were like that. That's the difference today. Most shops had boys to clean the fronts in the morning, the brasswork was done, the pavements washed.
The *lein fach*, (Devils Bridge Railway), had its own station where the Crosville Garage is now. Mr Hamer was the station master. When I worked for the grocer, on a Monday the farmers came up from the Rheidol Valley. I'd go down to the station with my truck and a parcel, and they'd put the parcel off at one of the halts and there'd be a pony and trap waiting. That's how they delivered. My grocer would be buying eggs and butter from the farmers and the farmers would buy

their goods from him. Evan Jenkins went bankrupt in the end.

When I was fourteen I came out of school and had a job on the prom. I was a steelbender's mate. There were about sixty of us building the promenade from south Marine Terrace to the wooden jetty. It took twelve months during 1930-1931. It was local labour, a shilling an hour. I'm the only one left. All the steel was bent by hand. The cement was brought in by ship, stored in the sheds and the men used to carry it down. I remember the *lein fach* running along the harbour, but not in use.

Evan Andrew, born 1916

Cambrian News

I worked for the *Cambrian News* for forty odd years. I first started as a compositor before the war. The *Cambrian News* was in Terrace Road then. The wages for a seven-year apprenticeship were five shillings a week in the first year then six shillings, seven shillings and sixpence, eleven shillings, fifteen shillings and finished on twenty-one shillings. I started when I was fourteen or fifteen. When I first started in the *Cambrian News* I was getting five shillings a week. I used to get a one shilling back from my mother to spend.

Like a few million others I was called up. I came out in 1945 and worked at my old job for six or seven months and then was appointed manager. We moved up to Grays Inn Road because we were expanding all the time, the premises in Terrace Road weren't big enough and everybody was on top of one another. During the move the paper didn't fail to come out once. In addition to that, the *Cambrian News* as a company did not own the premises. They were paying rent to W.H. Smith who owned the building. In Queen

Workmen engaged on building the promenade extension.

Street we bought the old warehouse of M.H. Davis and became our own landlord. This was important, in so far as if you went to the bank for a loan to buy a new machine for instance. In those days a new machine might cost £5,000 or £6,000. That was a lot of money then. If you had bricks and mortar as co-lateral you could get the money no trouble at all. The *Cambrian News* had premises in Mill Street too. That was the Art Bindery, we had a lot of people working down there. It was quite a thriving business, binding books and so on. Magazines were being printed every week and they had to be bound up into yearly volumes.

We had a contract with the National Library, the County Council, Theological College and various bodies like that. I think I'm right in saying we had one hundred and seventy staff when I finished, that was sixteen years ago [1983] when I was sixty-six.

Eric Evans, born 1917

Mid Wales Dairies

I left school in 1944 and went to work on a milk round as a milk boy. It's where the Indian Restaurant is now opposite Downie's Vaults. Mid Wales Dairy it was then. They had just lost a son in D-Day. It was a sad time when I started there.

I started off working with the boss, but ended up going round by myself. Everybody only had two pints a week, milk was rationed.

I had a truck with a big brass churn and a handcan. People used to leave their jugs on the doorstep.

The town was zoned because of rationing. You weren't allowed to go outside your zone. People had to buy their milk from you if they wanted to or not. You lost some customers and gained some because of the way it was shared out in zones. Our zone was New Street, Pier Street, Great Darkgate Street from the fish shop towards the castle, Laura Place, the promenade down to just the other side of the Belle Vue, Vulcan Street, past the Albion, Princess Street around the market and to the top of Bridge Street. Only a couple of hours it took. Milk was fourpence a pint. On Saturdays I'd knock the door to get paid and Christmas Day. You made sure to go round on Christmas Day to get the tips. The only day I never went round was Boxing Day.

You had to watch the truck didn't tip over. It tipped over with me in Pier Street and seventeen gallons went down the drain. There were two big wheels at the back and all the weight was on these. I left it with the two wheels against the gutter. We had to go cap in hand to other dairies as milk was all rationed.

I was there until 1946 and then I went as an apprentice to Mr Griffiths who was a plumber and started learning my trade. I went to the RAF then in 1948. I was out about five days before the Korean War started.

Ted Salmon, born 1930

The Coliseum

I was there from about 1935 until about 1941. I ended up as the projectionist in the old operating box. You couldn't get people to work for you with the war. They were either very young, which was unusual, or they were people over fifty. Even then it was a job to get them, as nearly all men about the fifty mark were in the AFS, the Special Constabulary, the Home Guard or the Emergency Fire Brigade, so they were committed after their working time to doing a shift at night with these various things. You had to do it then during the war so I was stuck there until 1941. My health was deteriorating. Everything was closed up in the projection room. The arc lamps were burning carbon to provide the light for the film. Of course with everything being cluttered up there was no way the fumes could get out, so you were breathing the fumes all the time. This got on my chest and my mother took me to the doctor. He said 'Get him out of there. He'll be in a sanatorium.' So I had to leave there and I went on the railway as a cleaner with the *Great Western Railway*.

Roger James, born 1926

An advertisement for Mid Wales Dairies, c. 1935.

A Shilling a Time

When you were grown up, when you were fourteen, you'd go to the station to carry bags. You used to earn more money than your father did. You were getting a shilling a time off the visitors. Sometimes you'd take them a long way and get a bit more. Old Potts used to chase you because it was really his job to carry bags.

Watty Chamberlain, born 1906

Great Western Railway

The way the system worked then on the old *Great Western Railway* was that the driver had to know the road. So an Aberystwyth driver would know, say the road to Carmarthen, from here to Shrewsbury and from here to Oswestry. If he had to take the train further they used to have a pilotman, a man who knew the road to say Birmingham, so he'd take charge with the driver of the train and he'd take it through to Birmingham. The same coming back. They were very, very safety conscious.

The railway here in my time employed about a hundred and seventy-eight staff between the goods yard, the parcel side of it, the passenger trains and the goods trains. The loco shed employed seventy to seventy-five. There were cleaners, firemen, drivers, office staff, fire droppers, coalmen, shed cleaners, boiler washers, fitters, and locomotive fitters. All that has gone now.

Water was a big thing for the old steam locomotives. Just where the old gasworks used to be, they used to pump water from the well and that used to supply the big tank where the old locomotive shed was. There was a big tank there that supplied the hydrants where you filled the tenders. It was necessary to have a water fitter and a water fitter's mate. Not that they had much to do. That meant that they would be free to do other things, say around the station. All in

all the footplate crew all got on well with everybody else.

Jack Johns, the driver, was the mayor of the town twice, in the days when you had a borough council that meant something. Ernie Roberts the station master was mayor twice. He served on the council for donkeys years and was an Alderman.

Roger James, born 1926

Pickfords

I left school to go to work in Pickfords, the photographers. Mr Pickford had a shop in Pier Street. I used to help in the office doing accounts at one time. Then I went upstairs and was doing the enlarging and the wedding photos. There were a crowd from school working in the summer because they used to take all the films from chemists, some right in the country. I had to keep count, pack them and send the bills out. I finished there because the war came and there wasn't the work.

Florrie Bevan, born 1916

The Laundry

I had to do war work or sign up. My father wouldn't sign the papers for me to go to the Air Force. I went in to the laundry in Mill Street doing war work. I was there four years, a terrible time working from eight in the morning to eight or nine at night. I was in the packing and sorting. That was because I'd worked in a shop and knew how to do it. It was the men who were in the wash-house.

Mavis Lowe, born 1924

Folding Uniforms

I went to work in the laundry where the car park is now. They were doing work for the army and air force. They had a separate place down underneath for the army work. We had to fold the officers' shirts, uniforms and such like. They went on a press and then you had to finish them by hand. A lot came from Tonfannau. There were a crowd working there. I enjoyed it. We started eight o'clock in the morning, sometimes 'til eight at night. The pay wasn't that exciting. There were mainly women there, a few men on the machines.

Florrie Bevan, born 1916

Queens Hotel

I worked in Broad Street, Birmingham, in a cafe by the waterworks. I said to a friend that I was fed up with this job. She said I should go and see an agent and ask him to get me a job by the sea and go for the summer. That's it, I came and I'm still here. I first came to Aberystwyth in 1930, the week the two battleships *Renown* and *Repulse* were in the bay. I worked in the Queens Hotel, a beautiful hotel. I was housemaid and waitress, I used to work whenever they were busy. It was a lot of hard work as there weren't all the different facilities for cleaning that there are today.

There was a lovely ballroom and I helped behind the bar there. A man named Mr Chapman used to run the hotel. It was a really posh hotel with a nice class of people. In the summer, after the evening dinner, there was a band used to come and play. Townspeople used to sit on the railings and listen to the music. Aberystwyth was better then than it is today. There used to be dances, dinners and down underneath, were tea rooms, which were open to the public. On the front of the building there were steps which led down to the bar and I used to help there. I can remember there was a first, second and third floor, but I don't remember how many bedrooms were there. We had to wear a waitress's uniform and everything. They used to bake their own bread. It was a Mr Slater who came from Birmingham who baked the bread. His grandson has got Slater's bread shop. In the kitchen there was a head chef and two other chefs. Most of the staff came from outside Aberystwyth for a season's work. I stayed on in the winter because hot and cold running water was put in that winter so I stayed on to help out. I went away to different hotels and came back. Amy Johnson stayed there when I was working there.

Winifred Lavin, born 1908

The Brewery

Mr Henry [Roberts] was foreman over all the workmen. George Fossett [Roberts] was in charge of the office staff.

They started making ice for the hospital and for ice cream. Then they had a plant to chill the beer to three degrees below freezing point and bottled it with a siphon filler. We used to pump the beer into the chiller to three degrees below freezing point. Then it went through filters, and then through the bottling machine. Crown Ale was the bitter and the Pale Ale was IPA. It was only that carbon dioxide was being put in to them to make them fizzy. We put about ten or twelve pounds of that in.

About 1930, after sales picked up a bit,

Mill Street, the laundry is in the centre of the picture.

they had a proper filler put in and a big washing machine for the bottles. Before that, they used to get all the bottles from the other side where they had the stout and Bass and things. When they had a new filler, we started bottling the stout as well, as the filler was quicker. Crown Ale was brought out in anticipation of the coronation of King Edward VIII and was kept on for a long time.

The one side of the brewery was the bottling plant, where they used to bottle Bass, Worthingtons and Barley Wine; then there was the cooper's place and a boilerhouse where my brother worked. Up above, there was a brewhouse where Jimmy James and Dai Bitchell worked. They used to start early in the morning, and then call Mr Henry [Roberts] about six o'clock to do the brewing. He was the brewer. With ordinary beers, we used to run them down into a cask, put them onto a stand and taste them to see if they were casky or not. There were two men down

in the cellar putting it into casks. All wooden casks in those days. Tom Thomas from Cilgerran was the cooper. He used to build the barrels up. He'd get a barrel and when that was starting to go, he'd cut it down to a [kilder] kin, then from a kin to a firkin, then from a firkin to a pin. When that was finished then he'd make a thing for washing dishes.

They started doing the brown ale about 1928, a couple of years before I started. Crown tops came in about 1932. They had six girls working there then. Before that, because of the siphon filler, you had to work two shifts. You were starting at six in the night and working eight hours. Before you'd done that, you'd started at seven, stopped for breakfast from eight to half past, had your own dinner and tea and carry on working 'til three in the morning, then start working again at seven. We had a new filler then. The bottles went round on a conveyer belt and we just had to watch it. They put the crown stoppers on the top. Before that, it was screw tops for Crown Ale and IPA.

I went in the end to spirits. I worked on the boiler, down the cellar. I think I worked everywhere, I worked on bottling the guinness and stout. At the end I worked in wines and spirits. You know the bragdy, the building next to the Black Horse? That's where they used to put the grains in to get them for brewing. They used to have it from Llanrhystud, then they got them from England, as well as the hops.

We worked eight 'til one on Saturdays. We started at seven, went for breakfast at eight 'til half past eight – most of the men lived in Trefechan, a break at eleven o'clock, then lunch from one 'til two and finish at five. I never tasted the beer, just to test and spit it out to see that it wasn't casky.

We were keeping Tonfannau going, taking beer out to the troops there. When they cut back, we were having more of an allowance than they were in south Wales, so we were supplying the pubs in Glynneath for about six or twelve months.

They were very good bosses, wonderful people. With Sir George, if you went in the office and he asked you something, you had to answer yes or no, not I don't know or I think. He wouldn't have none of that. He was a colonel in the Cardigan Battery before the First World War. After that he was made 'a Sir'.

If I wanted a day off, I'd go and find Mr Henry and say it was a lovely day for rabbiting, and the old man would give me half a crown to take his son out with me. I used to teach him to make rabbit nets. His

Dining Room of the Queens Hotel, c. 1930.

48

The bottling plant at Roberts Brewery.

father used to say, if he's as clever as that he can go to Llandovery College.

There was a welsh terrier there. The men had cans with an allowance of two pints of beer a day, and used to leave them on top of the cellar steps. They were like cans you carried tea in with a top. They were going down so much each day and one was blaming the other. One day they saw the terrier going down towards the lorries from one side to the other. He'd been drinking the beer and all the men had been blaming each other.

Watty Chamberlain, born 1906

Rocket Stout and Crown Ale

My father went to work for the brewery as a handyman, nothing to do with the brewing. Eventually I went to work there too. They used to employ six decorators to see to all the public houses out in the country that they owned. When I went there, there was only a foreman and two painters. I was treated like a

lord there. I couldn't go wrong with Mr Blake, the director. Whenever he came, say I was working in Aberdyfi, he'd always come and say, 'Where's White?' Then I'd have to test his Rocket Stout and then the Crown Ale and that. You daren't leave him because he needed your company. Many a time I was under the weather because I couldn't drink all the stuff what he could.

Reg White, born 1915

Madame Hedge

I worked in a shop for five years in Terrace Road, Madame Hedge it was then, a very posh fashion shop. Newman's fish shop used to be there. It had Madame Hedge on the top and just a few things in the window. Hassall's shop, another draper was next door. I dressed the windows and served customers. Thirty shillings a week I was getting. In at nine and finish at five. There was a little shop in Eastgate and I used to go there and pay three

Brewery workers, c. 1935

shillings and sixpence a week for a pot of tea. Saturday I worked from five until nine. I lived in Llanbadarn. There were no buses so I had to walk back and fore. I was always afraid passing the gasworks. There were no houses on the fields there, no Padarn Crescent.

Doris Price

The Family Business

I left school at fifteen and went in to the business. I'd been mucking about in the business since I was about ten years old doing menial jobs. Photography was very labour intensive in those days. Every print had to be handled, printed, developed, fixed, washed, dried, then sorted into its proper order particularly with the developing and printing trade. That work came after I went into the

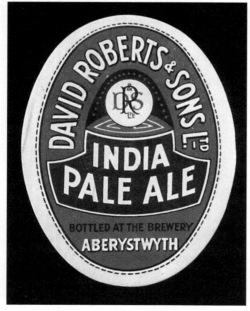

Pale Ale label.

business. I was going out photographing on a motorbike at fourteen. I was allowed to have a licence at fourteen in those days. I got me a motorbike and used to go and photograph camps in Clarach, scout camps and that sort of thing, with all the paraphernalia strapped to my back. It was Stan cameras in those days. I used to take the prints out, then get orders, that kind of thing. That went on for a bit, then I went to London more or less to get letters after my name. There was a Professional Photographers Association. My father was very keen to have this thing on the wall so he wanted me to qualify. It was roughly a City & Guilds. I did it in about six weeks as I knew so much at the time. This was attached to the Kodak works out at Harrow. That's how I qualified. We were still using Stan cameras for most of the stuff then. I got a large press camera, what the press boys had in that age. That took either a quarter plate or a twelve by nine centimetre flat film plate. Film was just coming in. We were the pioneers of flat film in this area. Everything was on glass plates up to then. This was very early 1920s.

Glynne Pickford, born 1909

College Hall Fire

One of the first scoops I had was the College Hall fire on North Road, all glass and timber. It was a Sunday afternoon and I was in the shop for some reason. The phone rang and it was a friend of mine phoning from the bottom of Queens Road. 'Do you know the College Hall is on fire?' I said no. 'Its going like blazes' he said. I jumped on my motorbike and went up to North Road and got my camera ready. I jumped up onto a wall and for some reason I put the camera that

52

College College Hall fire, 1933. This is one of the postcards sold at Mr Pickfords shop.

way up, and as I did that the roof fell in, and a cloud of sparks and fire went up in the air and I got a beautiful picture. I got a lot of others, many of which have been published since. The interesting part from my point of view was that I rushed back to the shop, developed the plates and got in touch with my father. He said we had a scoop here, I'll take them to Manchester. We got ten by twelve enlargments, and dried them quickly between two sheets of blotting paper. He and a friend went to Manchester. We had the front page of the *Daily Mirror* for which we had twenty-five pounds. They went round the other offices, *Daily Sketch* was going in those days, the *News Chronicle,* and the *Express.* He got around them all and they all used our photographs. One of them had the whole front page. I then went into the darkroom and started printing postcards and on Monday morning they were in the window. In the first two or three days we sold two thousand. They were taking them wet, they wouldn't even let them dry. Sixpence each. I got quite a few pictures in the papers but this was the only time I got the whole front page.

Glynne Pickford, born 1909

Dangerous Jobs

Some of the jobs I did were quite dangerous. There was something wrong with the roof of one of the gasometers in Llanbadarn. There were two then. Anyway they filled the one up to its maximum height and the only way of getting up on the top, was up the iron ladder on the outside. I put all my camera stuff in a rucksack on my back, I'd never been to that height before. I went right to the top, stood on top and took the photographs.

You know the war memorial on the castle? The figure on the top was on an orb and there was some trouble with it. They put up a very rickety scaffolding so they could examine it. Of course they wanted a photograph. I went up this rickety old scaffolding with my rucksack and photographed it.

I think the most hair raising one, was when they did the nose of the stone pier. They were taking the cement over in buckets. They had this very big crane there and at low tide they were tipping this quick drying cement at the base. They wanted to see some cracks but they couldn't get at it. They asked me if I'd photograph it. The only way I could do it, was if they put me in the bucket and swing me out. I was covered in cement but I got the photograph.

We sold thousands of postcards of the storm in 1938. I went down and took photographs on the first morning when the storm was at its height, on the corner by the Hotel Victoria, near the old police station. There was a man working in the shop and he came down with me. He was standing with his back to me because I couldn't stand up in the wind. I sold thousands of postcards of that. We sold them for sixpence.

Glynne Pickford, born 1909

CHAPTER 4

Entertainment

The Rink Cinema, Portland Street, 1923.

The Rink

The first cinema in Aberystwyth was the Rink. It was a wooden building between Salem chapel and those houses near the town hall. If it rained you needed a mackintosh. You could be sitting there and something would be rubbing against your feet and you'd find it was a rat. There was a corridor with a big wooden partition down one side. As kids we used to rush after school on a Wednesday to see the serial for a penny. Much to the annoyance of the proprietor, we would climb on top of this partition to whip our horse up. The rink was moved and the proprietor opened a cinema in Bath Street. That was where the old swimming baths was.

The films that made an impression when I was young, particularly in the old Rink, were the serials. You'd be watching the serial and see the hero thrown off a bridge in mid – air dropping down, and then it would come up 'Continued next week'. These were silent.

John Lewis, born 1913

First and Second house

It was all pictures then. You could go to first house, come out of that and go somewhere else, second house. I've seen people going to the big meetings in the chapels, the cwrddau mawr [big meetings] and if the minister was quick they'd go to second house. We went three or four times a week. It was only one shilling sixpence.

Olwen Penney

Above Peacocks

The Palladium was up above Peacocks in Market Street. Before Peacocks took it over it was a market hall and there were butchers and greengrocers, milliners and so on. Peacocks took it over and put a man named Hughes, who was a greengrocer in the market, in charge.

John Lewis, born 1913

Coliseum

The Coliseum was one of the central places to go. There'd be a man outside used to shout '*Clive of India*' or whatever film was showing at the time. We used to go to the cinema

every week. The Palladium was a cosy cinema. We used to go there on a Saturday. We used to have a sixpence, that was the matinee on a Saturday afternoon. You'd be left with someone hanging on by their fingertips until next week. We'd get so excited about it all. The cinema was always full, with both boys and girls. There was always shouting. The films were black and white. Some were silent.

Madge Richards, born 1908

First Talkie

The first talkie in Aberystwyth was in the old Imperial in Bath Street. *The Singing Fool* I think it was. There was a big queue to see it. The sound seemed more like an echo then the sound of today. It used to be sixpence to go to the cinema. If you went to the kids' matinee on a Saturday morning it was two pence ha'penny. The Pier never had a matinee, the Palladium, the Imperial and the Rink did matinees. Ninepence was an expensive seat. The most expensive seats were one shilling and threepence. All the cinemas charged the same. If I remember rightly when we used to run from school to the Rink to see the serial, we used to get in on a Wednesday afternoon for a penny.

John Lewis, born 1913

Palladium

We went to the cinema the night before the fire. It was a lovely cinema. I had a long scarf, green and white, Ardwyn colours, which I had knitted myself. My future husband was lodging in Grays Inn Road opposite the church. He brought me home, then a while after that he came round banging on the door and saying that the Palladium was on fire. I remembered then I'd left my scarf there.

Florrie Bevan, born 1916

Mrs Gale

Mrs Gale had long hair made in a bun. She used to sit counting the tickets and saying, 'Hello my darlings.'

Olwen Penney

Three Cinemas

The cinema was mostly full every night. There were three cinemas. There was the Forum, or the Imperial as it was known first in Bath Street; the Pier and the Coliseum. They were all doing well. A grown-up could go to the pictures for threepence. You didn't have the best seat in the cinema but you got in for threepence. Many people would go on Monday to the Coliseum, they'd go to the Imperial on a Tuesday and the Pier on a Wednesday. Most of the cinemas would change their programme on a Thursday. They would only hold a film for three days. Then it would be Coliseum again on a Thursday. You could be in the cinema every night of the week.

Roger James, born 1926

See You in the Tuppence Halfpennies

When I was in school we went to the Palladium every Saturday afternoon. The first three rows were two and a half pence.

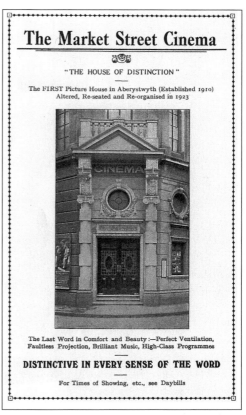

An *advertisement for the Palladium Cinema, Market Street, c. 1930.*

We used to shout at one another, 'See you in the tuppence halfpennies.' That was our weekly entertainment. Cowboys and things like that we wanted to watch.

Eric Evans, born 1917

Gipsy Smith

On the religious side, was when we had Gipsy Smith. I was about eleven years old. He came one year from America with a pianist. He was something like a Billy Graham in a way. The place was packed. I

Demolition of the ruins of the Palladium Cinema after the fire of 20 February 1935.

remember the school children having a holiday and coming from Penrhyncoch and Capel Seion and all those areas. We used to sit on the steps of this lovely stage with the Borough Choir singing behind. He used to tell us the story of how he was brought up. I can always remember us children crying and listening. Gipsy Smith had a big influence on me.

Gwladys Ednyfed Thomas

There To Pick Up Girls

The evangelist Gipsy Smith, he used to come before the war. He used to come to the College Hall where the bowling green is now. Gipsy Smith came here for a fortnight at the height of the season. He used to hold his Christian meetings and they were packed. People used to go to the front and be saved and such. We used to go there to pick up the girls and it used to be packed there, full up and the *hwyl* would be going.

Merfyn Jones, born 1919

Peace Pageant

In the pageant our group in school was Norway. I had long fair hair and curls. I had a black velvet cap. It was in the castle, a beautiful day.

Mavis Lowe, born 1924

Cor Y Castell

That was a big thing in the old days, when the miners were coming up here. You couldn't get passed on the prom there on a Sunday night unless it was raining.

Glynne Pickford, born 1909

Carnivals

There was a good carnival, third Wednesday in August, towards the end of the season and the schools starting to go back. Tourists were also starting to go back. Borth Carnival was a big thing, that was the first week in August. All the visitors were there then, and they used to have their tableaux and decorate their cars.

There would be perhaps twenty to twenty-five floats. A lot of people would be walking, mostly trying to be funny, doing Charlie Chaplin or looking like some film star.

Glynne Pickford, born 1909

Ellisons Entertainers

Where the putting green by the castle is now, first of all they had an iron framed building which they put canvas sides to, and a stage with lighting on. Ellisons Entertainers used to come every year. Uncle Tommy came afterwards. Some used to go on the bandstand. The earliest ones were on Elysian Grove where the houses are now. It must have been a hard life doing that.

Glynne Pickford, born 1909

Uncle Tommy's Minstrels

On the castle there used to be the pierrots. Uncle Tommy used to have shows there. He'd call you out of the audience to do a turn. He'd say a few jokes and be singing and dancing and clowning around. We thought it was great in those days. Mrs Twiddy who used to live in Cliff Terrace was with Uncle Tommy. She was a dancer and a singer. She used to wear shorts and as kids we used to think she was so pretty.

Mavis Lowe, born 1924

Billiards

There was a flourishing billiards and snooker league. There were the two Liberal Clubs, the Conservative Club, the YMCA, the Social Service Centre down in Trefechan, the Coopers; there were six or seven of these. You'd see about six chaps walking along the street about seven o'clock, with these long cases for their cues, going to wherever the fixture was. I can remember the great Joe Davies, the greatest player in the world coming down here for exhibitions. There were a number of local players who could give him a good game. The best local player was a chap called Tubby Pryse who was a very successful businessman with St Ivel Cheese. He became mayor and was a great swimmer.

Edward Ellis, born 1922

Coliseum

I remember quite a few big names coming here, to the Coliseum in the winter months. I think Gracie Fields came here. A chap named Saroni, like a popstar of those days, came and all the ladies went to see him. It was sixpence in the gods and you used to make paper arrows to throw at the people underneath. They were on for a week. Change of programme generally on a Thursday, nothing on a Sunday, except Cor Y Castell in the summer.

Glynne Pickford, born 1909

Football

Aber was a soccer town. Rugby only came in here after the Second World War. Aberystwyth Town had a well-established football side. In the 1930s there was a junior league with teams from Borth, Bow Street, Trefechan, the YMCA, the Liberal Club and more. It was a flourishing and important part of the life of the town. It gave great interest and activity to lots of young men and fierce rivalries developed. I remember there was a great succession of cup games between the Liberal Club and Trefechan, which went on from replay to replay, like a soap opera wondering what would the next episode be.

As far as the town football team was concerned, I played for them for a few years. About the fourth game I played for them was against Llanidloes on a Good Friday. There were well over two thousand, nearly three thousand watching. Llanidloes were the great rivals, a tremendous team. There was always a particular zip in the air when you played Llanidloes. There was a tremendous rivalry and respect on both sides. Sometimes it got a bit rough and ready. Football was a big thing. There weren't the opportunities for other sports in those days and it was supported by this junior league.

Edward Ellis, born 1922

The Fair

The fair in those days was in upper Great Darkgate Street. There weren't the amusements there are today, then it was all stalls. The first fair was a hiring fair, when they stood by the town clock and were hired for a year. They'd give them a shilling and that hired them for a year. Then there were the two fairs after that where just the stalls came. They still have the three now.

Glynne Pickford, born 1919

The Wall of Death

When the fair came every November, there would be stalls with army surplus – marvellous. Farmers would be there buying all the ex-army greatcoats and those leather things the troops used to wear, which were ideal for farms. There were earphones, ex-army radios which were rubbish but you could take the parts out of. The fair was more like the old hiring fair, not like it is today with rows of commercial stalls. This was late 1940s. At night, the Wall of Death was the most daring thing with a motorcycle and a very attractive scantily dressed young girl sitting on the handlebars, or sometimes a large dog. The other things were the boxing booths. If you wanted to have a go you got to go in free and if you lasted three rounds you got ten bob, but you'd have all hell knocked out of you. They were professional. A lot of local lads tried but I never saw anyone go three rounds.

A favourite of ours was where you had a wooden slot, you rolled a penny down it and at the far end of the stall there were little alcoves. One said win and one said lose and there would be one big prize say ten shillings. You had a good chance to get your money back or maybe win a sixpence.

Don Parker, born 1934

Coconut Shies

There were stalls, but not like it is at the moment. There were coconut shies and all sorts of odd things being sold. It was at the side of St Pauls church and around the old meat market and the upper part of Great Darkgate Street where they hold the market at the moment. There would be a roundabout of some sort at the top of Park Avenue. I suppose the fair stopped being at the top of town during the late twenties.

John Lewis, born 1913

Men on One Side, Girls on the Other.

I can remember the *ffair cyflogi*, the hiring fair. There would be men on one side of Great Darkgate Street and the girls on the other. Their contract would be for twelve months. The farmers then would vie to get the best deal they could. The girls were getting about twelve pounds a year and their keep, the men thirty to thirty-five pounds. The farmer would put a two shilling piece in the hand and that was binding for twelve months. That two shillings then was spent in the fair. That was Studts of course. There were big traction engines against the school wall. They supplied the electricity. It has altered now. There used to be coconut shies, you don't see them today. There also used to be the boxing booth – the farmers' boys would be down there and have a bash. The tough guys from south Wales would be there. You got a pound if you could last three rounds; not many did. All the way down both sides of Smithfield Road, as it was before being called Park Avenue, there'd be all the stalls with hurricane

Community Hymn Singing in the castle grounds, c. 1940.

Participants in the Peace Pageant held in the castle grounds, 1935.

lamps. There might be someone selling lino, we didn't have carpets in them days. Another would be selling crockery and shouting, they don't seem to shout today like they did then. Number eight rock came in after the war. If we had money to spend, it was the swings or the dodgems if they were there. We'd go in to see the boxing, which was about sixpence.

Evan Andrew, born 1916

New Year Dances in the Pier

In 1934 I came to Aberystwyth and met my husband Ralph who played in his father's dance band and we became sweethearts. I came to Aber over Christmas and New Year and having lived always in London the contrast between celebrating the New Year in London and Aberystwyth was so terrific. Aberystwyth was a small town and it was so different from London. I remember coming from Paddington in the good old steam trains; they were so comfortable and lovely and packed with young people from Aberystwyth. In those days young people had to go to big cities like London and Manchester to find work. But like homing pigeons they came home to roost at Christmas and New Year. Everybody knew each other and I was always so struck by the cheerfulness of people on the railway. It was bustling. Aberystwyth was a self-contained little town and the same family continued lived in the houses, not like today. Every one of them was full and there were generations of people living in those houses.

It was a close-knit community. It was a bustling little town and of course the shops were so different.

The Pier was the social centre of Aberystwyth. Because of Evered's dance band and his strict tempo and because we all listened to the wireless and were familiar with Jack Payne, Henry Hall, Here's to the Next Time, Joe Loss and eventually Victor Sylvester, we knew all the tunes. The dancers of Aberystwyth were very proficient because they had the schooling with Evered's band – strict dance tempo. He would be there, he played the piano of course, a little elevated and he would set the pace. It was a very romantic period and I was a romantic. These 1930s New Years Eves meant so much to me

Young people came to dances in long dresses. Money was scarce in those days. There was a depression although we were not aware of it because we didn't have television and we weren't alerted every hour to the news. The young women who had come from, say south Wales to work in hotels and guest houses, earned very little money, but they saved up. We were softened as to what was really going on. They went to London at the end of September when Aberystwyth would have its main holiday, because the season was over, and bought their dresses then. They bought them from Oxford Street in guinea shops. They were just a guinea but it was a relative value because a guinea was quite a lot of money and some men only received two pounds a week to bring up a family. The dresses were very stylish and perhaps they wouldn't buy one every year. There were lots of satins cut on the cross, very sleek. You had to be very slim to wear them, but many wore them regardless. They were very clinging, went

Ellisons Entertainers were a popular troupe of entertainers for many summer seasons during the 1920s and 1930s.

UNCLE TOMMY'S MINSTRELS 1939

Uncle Tommy's Minstrels superseded Ellisons Entertainers and are fondly remembered by many townspeople for their antics in the castle grounds.

down to the ground, sleeveless of course with a strap and lots of diamantes, very beautiful. I didn't go in for the slinky ones, I just wasn't the type. I remember New Year 1935, I had a white dress with little pink rose buds. I still have the letter Ralph wrote to me. He said I never notice what anyone is wearing, but you looked absolutely lovely in your white dress. My heart missed a beat.

You'd come along this long passage. On the right was the powder room where you'd hang your coats. For the girls it was the time of the permanent wave and in order to maintain it there would be kirby grips put at intervals. Actually I was lucky, because we could wear them. I had a young lady from Aberystwyth whose father was the shoe repairer in Chalybeate Street and she had a place in Gerrard Street, which is now of course in the Chinese quarter. They didn't encourage the use of kirby grips in London,

but here, I suppose because of the wind and the weather, they wore them.

I can remember lots of the perfumes, it wasn't Eau de Toilette as it is now, it was the real McCoy. It was California Poppy, horrible, very pungent. It wasn't what I'd choose. You could buy it in Woolworths. It was a heavy smell you'd remember. I liked Gardenia. There was a lot of makeup worn – lipstick and rouge. People really did their best. They really made an effort.

Many came from outside [Aberystwyth] by coach. There were lots of single girls who didn't have partners and lots who came with their partners. They would arrive at about quarter to eight because the dance started at eight and Evered was right on the ball. He would give the sign, the band would strike up and they were off. They played quicksteps, slow foxtrots and romantic waltzes. Everybody liked quicksteps as people could really let rip. They had dances which everyone could do, like the conga. There was an 'excuse me dance' which was very, very popular. That was the time when those who were sitting there without a male escort would have a partner and maybe a friendship would be struck up. For those who had partners, it was a nice excuse for them to change partners. As the song says, 'will you change partners and dance with me?' that's what it was you see. To the left of the band, almost secreted under the stairs, there was a little circle of people, business people and their wives. They were like chaperones watching what was going on. When the waltz came and the lights dimmed they would venture on to the floor. They had a hokey-cokey and 'doing the

lambeth walk' with great shouts. The more flamboyant took to the floor with great strides and panache for the tango. Ralph would accompany them on the accordion to give local colour.

Some of the men would be in evening dress and some just in suits. The Pier would be decorated with streamers and things, and secreted in the corner were balloons for the magic moment. There was a cafe as you came in and a soda fountain. They had knickerbocker glories second to none, and during the evening there would be an interval and there was a balcony and you could look down. It was like a cauldron. When it came to the interval people would go upstairs for their refreshments. The band would have a rest. Twenty minutes later and

L. Evered Davies Danceband at the Pier, c. 1938. On the double bass is Reg White.

Ralph Davies, c. 1935.

Evered was back on the stand, they were very disciplined. Some went out for a little stroll to get the air. The evening went by so quickly. Dances resumed, there was the Veleta, a barn dance with lots of stamping, that sort of atmosphere As the evening wore on there were high spirits and it was an atmosphere of great joy. The Pier was second to none as it had a sprung dance floor, a great departure from the old Parish Hall. Everybody knew everybody and if they hadn't known them at the beginning they did at the end. It was that sort of atmosphere. Everybody had the chance to join in. There was drink in the Pier bar but Evered had a rule of his own. After ten o'clock people were not allowed in to the

dance unless they had a ticket or a pass because he didn't want any unseemly behaviour to spoil the rest of the dances. They did have a drink, but people didn't drink in those days like they do now.

Later, you could see the men with their watches thinking was time was getting on. Evered, the band leader, was standing with his stop watch, a roll of the drums and Happy New Year! Bursts of clapping, lots of kissing and cuddling. Then with great gusto *Auld Lang Syne*. It was a memorable time, it really was. If the New Year fell on a Saturday the dance would finish at quarter to twelve because of the next day being Sunday. On the other times, one o'clock. People were flagging a little bit; when you think it was

Mrs Violet Davies, c. 1935.

on from eight to one – five hours. The time would come and Evered would say, take your partners for the last waltz and they would play, '*Who's taking you home tonight?*' Of course those arrangements had been made and everyone knew who was taking who home. And then, I'm talking about the 1930s, it was *God Save the King*. Then lots of cheering for the band.

I remember the people walking in the streets and the murmuring of voices on the way home. There was no fear you could walk home alone.

Violet Davies

Evered Davies, bandleader and photographer.

Evered Davies Band with Ralph as bandleader 1947. Second from the right is Ronnie Hughes the trumpeter.

CHAPTER 5

War Memories

Evacuees with gas masks and labels outside Aberystwyth Railway Station.

First World War

Old Contemptibles

In August 1914 when war started, there were a great number of troops here, Territorials and they were at Lovesgrove. The war must have come on us very suddenly and they were all mustered straight away and I can remember them marching through the town cheering, flags flying and bands playing. They thought they were going on holiday. They were what was known as the Old Contemptibles. I was five; that's the first thing I can really remember.

Glynne Pickford, born 1909

Billets and Brass Buttons

When the First World War broke out we had soldiers billeted with us. I can remember

Troops leaving Aberystwyth on the outbreak of the First World War, 1914.

they had brass buttons on their coats and I can remember them polishing these buttons. Everybody had to take them. We had two or three in our house. Young boys they were, but men to us as we were young children. The nicest one was Harvey. He wrote to us. I don't know whether he got out of the war. They were drilling them outside where the old National School was. They used to shout at them. We felt quite sorry for them really and they were young when you look back, nice boys. They'd do their training and move on elsewhere. We had to make room for them, there was no option.

Madge Richards, born 1908

Marching At Night

They had to separate the Cheshires and the Royal Welsh. They were always fighting here. They were having route marches at night instead of getting down into pubs and things.

Watty Chamberlain, born 1906

Theological College

I remember the Theo College was converted into a military hospital. I remember the casualties being brought in there, they were in a blue uniform. They were taken out of their military uniform and put into a blue uniform, flannelette material, no cut to it at all, it just sat on them. My father arranged concerts for them and used to do what was called Black Magic. That was a little stage with very bright lights right round it. My father would come in with a vase and put it on a table. Without anyone else seeing, this

69

man who was all in black, face and everything, would come in and get hold of this vase and put it on another table. My father would go and try and pick it up, but it had gone. It was comedy stuff to try and make the boys laugh. Some of them had lost legs and hands and were in a very bad way; some of them were walking around the town with sticks.

Glynne Pickford, born 1909

The Rink

As a young boy we used to stay outside the Rink in Bath Street. The Yanks were here and they used to treat us to go in. It used to cost a penny. It was just before the end of the war.

Watty Chamberlain, born 1906

The End of the War

Towards the end of the war I'd graduated to a little boys bike. I was coming ten when the war ended and I remember going round the countryside to Glanyrafon where we used to know the people there. I used to go as far as that and they'd give me a few potatoes, a couple of eggs or a corner of butter. Things were so short. It was wonderful that a child of nine years old could do that, you wouldn't be able to do that today, the traffic wouldn't allow it. I remember the big hullabaloo when the war finished, everybody on the prom and letting maroons off, that kind of thing. There were street parties. We managed to get food together somehow. Food was very short, but never as short as it was in the big cities.

Glynne Pickford, born 1909

Wounded soldiers in their characteristic uniforms outside the Theological College, c. 1917.

Second World War

Becoming an Evacuee

We all met outside the school in Liverpool. If you had an older brother or sister you went with them. We walked to the station in Liverpool and all got on the train. We had a gas mask and our names and everything pinned on us.

Nora Elwill, born 1928

Bring Me Back a Parrot

My brother and I came here on 2nd September 1939, the day before the war started. We were evacuated with our school. I lived in a district of Liverpool called Everton and went to Lorraine Street School. I'd only just started because I was just four and a half years old. The whole school was evacuated on 2nd September and we came here by train from Liverpool with the rest of the school. My brother was seven. I'd never been on a train before. I remember the part I didn't like was going into tunnels, but my brother looked after me very well, he wasn't scared. He's always been the sensible one.

When we were waiting for the train, hundreds and hundreds of children, a policeman came up to us and asked us to bring back a parrot, as though we were going to a foreign country. We all had our labels fastened onto our coats, tied on to the lapel with your name and address on, and gas masks in cardboard boxes. My brother and myself also had little haversacks an uncle of mine had made. Today there would be a national outcry if

you sent children away from home as under equipped as that and not knowing where they were going to go, no parents with them, just teachers.

Don Parker, born 1934

Carnation, Corned Beef and Chocolate

I was evacuated with a school I didn't go to. In 1938 I moved from an infants school to a junior school, but not the school that my mother wanted me to go to. When we were evacuated it was with the school I couldn't get into. Nobody was being evacuated with the school I was going to so I didn't know the boys or girls I was being evacuated with. We got on the train in Liverpool early in the morning, with little labels to denote where we were from. We got as far as Borth, got off the train and went into the field opposite the station which had a marquee. I'd never seen such wide, open spaces before, I was only nine. The doctor checked us over. They gave us a packet of cornflakes, a tin of Carnation condensed milk, a tin of corned beef, a big bar of chocolate and a carrier bag to put it all in.

Ted Salmon, born 1930

Church Hall

When we got to Aberystwyth we went from the station to the church hall and in the church hall we were all given a parcel with Lincoln biscuits. People came then and picked us. 'We'll have so many in our house.' We came to Rheidol Terrace. Coming from Liverpool, you can't imagine what it was like to go to the front, to see the sea of a morning when you woke up; it was just brilliant. There were no cars on the prom and we loved the castle grounds.

Nora Elwill, born 1928

The Scene at the Station

I remember my mother taking me down and standing alongside the school wall and watching all these children coming off the train. My mother had explained that because of the bombing in the big cities it wasn't safe for them to be there, and they had left their parents to come to Aberystwyth to be in a safer place.

Pam Evans

Borth

My first recollection of Aberystwyth was when we arrived, well no actually we didn't arrive in Aberystwyth. The train stopped in Borth for some reason or another. Now I've been told it was because they were worried about congestion around Aberystwyth Station, so it put in at Borth. We got off on the platform at Borth and there were various people about. They were handing each of the evacuees a carrier bag and you had simple supplies, a pound block of Cadbury's chocolate, a tin of corned beef, a packet of biscuits, a tin of condensed milk and various things like that, which you were to take with you wherever you were going.

Don Parker, born 1934

A Rolls Royce Home

We got off the train in Borth after leaving Liverpool. We were taken by bus from Borth to Chancery School and once in Chancery School we were made to sit behind desks. While we were there people were coming in and walking up and down

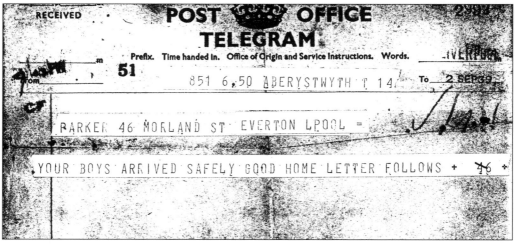

The telegram sent by Don Parker and his brother shortly after arriving in Llanfarian, 1939.

and saying 'I'll have you'. The only thing I remember was a lady standing in front of us and saying 'Will you two little boys come with me?' We were taken home. I'd never been in a car before and it was a big Rolls Royce belonging to Smiths of Ffosrhydygaled. They'd lent it to help out and we were taken to Figure Four, Llanfarian to the home of David and Anne Jane Edwards. They were to become my foster parents. The first thing they did was take us across to the post office and we sent a telegram to my father and grandmother. My mother had died in 1938, so I was living with my father and my grandparents. We sent a telegram telling them we were safe and in a good home and would send a letter later. The only thing else I can remember about that day was taking my carrier bag to bed with me. I didn't want anybody pinching my block of chocolate.

Don Parker, born 1934

No Organization

We had evacuees during the war, they were lovely. They came at ten o'clock at night. They just planted them late at night. There was no organization. Several children came and never went back. They were only six years old, pretty little children too. We weren't supposed to have them really, but the lady next door couldn't take them. She had visitors or something. I was up all that night making dresses for them as they'd got chocolate over everything. They loved it here. They used to go outside and say 'Eeeh what a grand house.'

Madge Richards, born 1908

Llanfarian

From Borth we were put on a bus and arrived in Llanfarian. We were all put in the village hall and picked out. The people who picked me were Mr and Mrs Evan Griffiths. He was a plumber. He lived then opposite the hall on the main road. I remember crying the first night. I didn't know where the hell I was. My sister had gone to Colwyn Bay, she was evacuated with her school.

Ted Salmon, born 1930

Enjoying Themselves

Two of the children who were with me didn't know what beds were. They were going to sleep on the floor. They were nice little children and I think they enjoyed themselves.

Doris Price

Declaration of War

The next day everything went very quiet in the house. I remember sitting on Uncle Dai's knee and hearing the Prime Minister saying that war had been declared. We were very lucky, we had wonderful foster parents. They looked after us like their own children.

Don Parker, born 1934

From Scotland Road

We had three evacuees from the Scotland Road area of Liverpool and they were poor. They were with us for about a month, then their mother came to pick them up with two

Evacuees at Llanfarian. Ted Salmon is on the extreme left of the back row, c. 1943.

more children. They'd have been better staying in Aber for a while. They didn't have any nightdresses or anything. People were sewing anything up trying to clothe them. I remember little Eileen, the middle one, her toenails were growing into her skin. One night I put her to bed and cut her toenails and she put her arms round me and kissed me and kissed me.

Olwen Penney

Still In Touch

One evacuee, a little girl, stayed behind and was with me for five years. She was eleven when she came. Her parents never wrote to her while she was with us, but as soon as she came of an age to go to work they sent for her back. She still writes to me now.

Doris Price

Brothers and Sisters

Brothers and sisters were kept together as much as possible. There were a few cases where they were split up but this was soon put right. If it was done, it was by accident. The next evacuees to us in Llanfarian were in the vicarage at Figure Four. The vicar had a family of four with him, two girls and two boys; two of them were twins. We had playmates within a hundred yards of us. I'm still in contact with half the family today.

Don Parker, born 1934

Anfield to Penparcau

Two of us came here but the other boy wasn't with us more than a month. His mother came and took him back. It was the time of the phoney war and nothing was

Don Parker with his foster parents, Mr and Mrs Edwards.

happening. We started in the old school in Penparcau in the afternoons. The local children were there from eight to twelve, we were one 'til five. That wasn't very satisfactory so they got us in the Neuadd Goffa. My old school, Anfield Road, wasn't very far from Liverpool football ground. We used to stand outside the house and collect cigarette cards on a Saturday afternoon and then go into the football.

Ted Salmon, born 1930

School

At first we went to Chancery School. Because there were both English and Welsh children there wasn't enough room; Chancery School is not a very big school. What happened at first was that the evacuees went to school in the morning, the Welsh children in the

Don Parker and his elder brother shortly after arriving in Llanfarian, 1939.

afternoon. After a short while all the English children in Chancery, the evacuees, were taken from there and sent to a school in Llanfarian Village Hall. Now we'd all have been dead in a day with the traffic. We were all over the road. Then there were only two cars in Llanfarian. The vicar and the local squire, who was Bert Matthews' father in Cwmcoedwig, each had one. You were lucky if you saw cars on the road at all.

Don Parker, born 1930

We Thought It Would Never End

I came to Aber in September 1939, the war had just started. All the twenty-ones had to join up. We ended up in the drill hall here, sleeping on the floor with nothing, just a blanket. It was ten or eleven o'clock at night when we got here. The following morning we went down to the slaughterhouse and that's where we had our meals. When they got it all sorted, we were sent to the Picton Hotel on the prom. That was alright. I was in the 146 Field Regiment, the Pembrokeshire Yeomanry. The officers used to have their mess in the big houses near the brewery, the lawn and the green. Sergeant Major White would come round after breakfast and walk us all round the prom. We thought it would never end.

We were free at nights and went to the pictures, the Coliseum mostly. There was nothing else to do. Our wages then when I joined were only fourteen shillings a week. That carried on nearly until I came out of the army. We moved from here to Llandudno. I was in Aber for about three months.

Bill Penney, born 1918

Jewish Evacuees

A lot of Jewish people were evacuated to Aberystwyth during the war. They made business connections in the town and sold jewellery and material, clothes and things like that. There was one, a furrier living next door to us. There were five or six Jewish families, Birmans, and Rosenbergs were some. They were very nice people, very kind and mixed very readily with the local people. They must have come here when I was leaving school, about 1939. The Birmans bought a house in North Road. There were two families of them. Their girls were about the same age as me. They went to the old National School in North Road. One is an actress who has been on TV, Rose Birman.

Roger James, born 1926

Mr and Mrs Bill Penney on their wedding day.

Llanfarian, c. 1935.

A Penny for the Bus.

We were in Neuadd Goffa for a couple of years. If it was wet, Mrs Griffiths would give us a penny to go on the bus. I didn't like going on the buses as they were always packed. There were no cars then, just buses every two hours or so. After a couple of years the number of evacuees started dwindling so they moved us from Penparcau and brought us to the hall; that was at the beginning of 1944. Numbers went down lower still and then they put us into the board school in Alexandra Road. We were mixed with the locals. During the war we didn't mix much with the locals, it was them and us. There was always mud fights and everything. That was because they were going to their school and we were going to our school. Some of the children here couldn't speak English. Mr and Mrs Griffiths didn't have children so they treated me like their son.

Ted Salmon, born 1930

Here for Five or Six Weeks

There was something wrong with one child, she couldn't walk and she was sick. My mother thought she wasn't used to rich food, like lamb and mint sauce. No one told us anything about them. Someone came round to see they were alright and my father mentioned this and she was taken off to hospital.

They were with us for five or six weeks then the mothers came and took their children home. One of them came down to see us when she was in her teens.

Madge Richards, born 1908

School in the Library

We first went to school in Alexandra Road and then after a few weeks we were put into separate classes and our school was transferred to the first floor in the library.

Playtime for us, when we were in the library, was to go down the stone steps and play on the jetty.

If it was nice in the morning, if the sun was shining, we'd go for walks up Constitution Hill, Borth, or Clarach. In the afternoons we'd go swimming, either at the other end of the prom or this end. We had lots of nature study lessons, collecting flowers and pressing them in books, things like that. We did a lot of going around the countryside with the school. It was beautiful and the people were lovely.

Nora Elwill, born 1928

In Isolation

Later, there was an epidemic of diphtheria with the evacuees. My sister and I both had diphtheria, we weren't actually ill with it but we got the germ, we were carriers, so we were put in Tanybwlch. Those were the best days of our lives, we loved it. We didn't want to come out of Tanybwlch. We used to play in the woods and go right along to the ruins of the summer house and play on the beach all day because we weren't ill. It was such a marvellous time in Tanybwlch.

After the war, when everyone was going on holiday to Spain. I always came to Aber because I loved it and my husband loved it.

Nora Elwill, born 1928

The Great Dictator

The Yanks gave us a party once in the Kings Hall. There were some Americans stationed in Aberaeron, in a camp on the hill, and they gave all the evacuees a party and a treat to the pictures. There was one film, *The Great Dictator*, with Charlie Chaplin, they took us to see that. It was in the Coliseum.

Ted Salmon, born 1930

Rationing

My father couldn't manage with the sugar; I stopped taking sugar and I've never taken it since. We used to go to the grocers to fetch the sugar. They used to make their own bag for the sugar to go in. Fascinating it was to watch them. They used to make this paper bag, then weigh it, so much for each of us. Mair, my younger sister, couldn't make her ration go, so we used to help each other out.

Madge Richards, born 1908

Tinned Bacon and Dried Eggs

I have vivid memories of having tinned bacon and dried egg. You couldn't get butter so you had to eke your margarine out. After the war it was very exciting to see a banana or an orange, as we'd never even seen fruit like that. I do remember that when you went out at night, everything was deadly dark. There were no lights and you had to make sure your windows were covered up before you put the light on.

Pam Evans

Sacks of Everything

There was rationing, but not as much as in Liverpool. We never went short of food.

Nora Elwill (third from left, back row) during her stay at the isolation hospital.

Where we lived, the lady used to buy everything in sacks, sacks of carrots, sacks of potatoes, hams and everything. She used to make 'stwmp' which was potatoes mixed with swede. It was beautiful. We used to have porridge with bread in, of a morning. We ate well. We were well looked after. For us evacuees the meals we got, well we just couldn't believe them. We had a dinner on a night and afterwards a sweet. They'd give us a baked apple or an apple crumble. We didn't realise what that was. At home we were just used to our dinner and that was it.

Nora Elwill, born 1928

Never Been Inside a Church

There was another little boy who stayed with the Watsons up the road. He was about six when he came and couldn't read or write or anything. They lavished attention on him and bought him all sorts of things and taught him to read. He could read his comics before he left there. They clothed him – when he came he was almost in rags. His mother was living with a man who wasn't his father. The Watsons got fond of him and would have adopted him if they could. When his parents came to fetch him back he had a suitcase full of things; when he came he had nothing to change into. It was such a pity, they were broken hearted when he left. They were Church of England and Mr Watson was warden in the Holy Trinity church. Mrs Watson took him to Trinity church and the choirboys were singing. He'd never been inside a church. He said in a loud voice, 'These choirboys give me bellyache.' Mrs Watson didn't know where to put herself.

Madge Richards, born 1908

Interned

The Second World War was a bit sad as a lot of the Italian men were interned. The women were alright and we had to carry on the business. Our shop was requisitioned by the army, but it caught fire. After a week the sergeant came and said to my mother, 'I think we had better give you the shop back Mrs Carpanini, you carry on.' We put it right and carried on from there. It was a bad time for Italian men as they loved this country but it was a fact that we weren't allies at that time. People were very kind to us just the same. We were just sorry that my father couldn't come back straight away. He was kept in the Isle of Man.

Leonora James

Coastguards

Dad was in the coastguards. He had to walk down as far as the limekiln at Morfa Bychan. Depending on the state of the tide he would walk over the cliffs and back along the beach or the other way around. Going north, he'd go as far as Borth, again over the cliffs one way and along the beach the other. That was done every day. They had to go in case there were any bodies washed up or anything. I think there were five or six coastguards altogether.

Pam Evans

A Garrison Town

I remember the boys coming from Dunkirk. Some were billeted in Trefechan, there's a plot up the road where the cars park now. They dug it all up one day to give them something to do and keep them occupied. They were here for a while. The town was a garrison town during the war. There were hundreds and hundreds of the air force here. The air force commandeered the hotels on the prom, The Queens, the Belle Vue, the Marine and the Lion Royal at the top of Great Darkgate Street. On a Wednesday, when we had a half day from the shop, we'd go on the prom to watch them training and parading. A lot of the army were billeted down in South Marine Terrace. They commandeered a lot of the big houses down there. They used to march under the bridge in batches to the drill hall every day for their food.

Mavis Lowe, born 1924

No Girls

I remember coming home on leave and the town was full of airforce blokes and we couldn't get any girls because they'd got them all.

Des Davies, born 1926

Men from 'B' Company 1st Cardiganshire Home Guard, c. 1940.

King's Hall Dances

The dances in the Kings Hall were marvellous. Ballroom dancing it was then, foxtrots and quicksteps and waltzes. Evered Davie's band used to be there. Friday night was the RAF dance, shilling to go in, but if you had your boyfriend with you they paid for you of course. The dances would finish about ten.

In all those years with the blackout, we'd be coming home from the pictures or after a dance and we'd meet many boys running past to get back to their billets on time. They'd wave and shout goodnight as they passed. There was never anyone attacked or robbed, nothing and there were thousands of boys here during the war. You could go home in the dark with no fear of anything.

Mavis Lowe, born 1924

BEF

In 1940 the British Expeditionary Force came here after Dunkirk. They were billeted around the town. We had two in our house. The BEF boys were here for quite a long time. My father had two of them fishing in the boat with him. They asked him for a job, otherwise they'd have to do jankers, peeling spuds and that. At that time there was a pillbox as you go down to the harbour. There were guards there and you had to have a pass to go down to the harbour. Some of these BEF men were on guard duty. The army was trying to find something for them to do, so they were doing all kinds of jobs, helping people out and that. I was still in school then.

Des Davies, born 1926

Billets

They used to mark the pillar on the side of your door with how many troops you would have billeted with you. My great-aunt had two, my grandmother six. I remember them exercising on the promenade and pulling themselves up the side of promenade with ropes. The Americans used to come round and if you were lucky they might give you a packet of chewing gum. Occasionally you'd see prisoners of war with either a round patch, a square or a triangle sewn on their backs. They came in with people from the farms where they worked.

I remember the mines going off out at sea and the shrapnel falling down on the roofs. One of the mines bashed against the rocks. A piece of shrapnel from that one

Coastguards outside their lookout, now demolished, on the castle grounds, c. 1942.

RAF personnel outside the White Horse Hotel. Third from left in the back row is Freddie Mills the noted boxer.

came through our bedroom window. Mainly they tried to get them into a safe place and detonate them. I can remember about half a dozen of them.

Pam Evans

Spitfires

Glenys Thomas, my foster mother's daughter was in the NAAFI. Her cousin, Katie Cooper, was in the WAF. Katie was a beautiful girl, really lovely and she was stationed in Aberporth. They lived on a farm called Troedyfoel. We went up there one day, I didn't know what for at the time but it was Katie's birthday. My brother and I were there and my foster mother and Glenys. Then a wonderful thing happened; there was a squadron of Spitfires stationed at Aberporth and two Spitfires came over, just above the farm and did a victory roll. They'd have been court martialled if they'd been caught. The thrill for two young boys to see these, they were maybe fifty feet in the air and the noise!

Don Parker, born 1934

Street Party in High Street to celebrate the end of the Second World War, 1945.

Street Party

When the war finished we had a street party
with long tables in the street. It was very
strange but whenever there was a street party
I was ill. I think I had chicken pox. All the
tables were trimmed and Mum made cakes.

Pam Evans

End of the War

All we had when we came home was two
quid, a certificate from the town and a Bible
from St Michaels church. That was it.

Des Davies, born 1926

CHAPTER 6

Personalities

Aberystwyth celebrities as caricatured by Matt of the Sunday Graphic, c. 1932.

Daunty Simmonds

The story we used to have of Daunty Simmonds, was that he was going around to one of the bigger houses in Llanbadarn Road, opposite the Vicarage Fields, was going and picking flowers in the front garden, then going around to the back door and selling them.

He was an old butler and used to wear a tailcoat always. I think he came from Llanbadarn way somewhere. All these characters used to turn out for the carnival.

Gwladys Ednyfed Thomas

Johnny Twtin

He used to go round town selling magazines like *Old Moores Almanack*. He used to deliver the *Cambrian News* and the *Welsh Gazette* on the days they came out. He'd have say two dozen copies of the *Cambrian New* to deliver, which might take him to South Road. Old Johnny was a big heavy bloke and a bit awkward on his feet. If you'd see him in South Road, he'd give you a halfpenny to go back to the *Cambrian News* and fetch some more papers to deliver.

Des Davies, born 1926

Every House and Every Resident

If you wanted to know where anybody lived in Aberystwyth, Johnny Twtin could tell you. He knew every house and every resident in Aberystwyth.

John Lewis

Ned y Lorne

Edward Davies was his proper name. His nickname came from his family having owned the sailing ship *Lorne*. He used to live in Prospect Street. He was a sort of assistant to the harbour master. When ships used to come into the harbour, there used to be capstans on the stone pier and the wooden jetty. If ships that were a bit long came into the harbour, we used to knuckle them round because they couldn't negotiate the bend into the harbour entrance. Ships like the *Grosvenor* couldn't negotiate the turn and had to be knuckled round. To help them, we'd put a headline from the wooden jetty and a stern line from the stone pier. There were two sheds on the wooden jetty. One was a shelter, the other was a shed where we kept the ropes and handspikes for the capstans and things like that. Ned y Lorne used to look after those. We had a light on the end of the wooden jetty. There was a mast where the light is on the stone pier. There was an oil light on that, which had to be lit every night. Ned y Lorne used to light it. On the bridge going to the stone pier there was another light. That brought you in until you got the light on the end of the wooden jetty abeam. Then you could come round and go straight up the river. Ned Y Lorne used to look after those. Supposing we were going to have a southerly gale, Ned would have to go down to the stone pier where there was another shed. Ned would have to get the cone up and hoist it up on the mast with the apex down. If it was going to be a northerly gale it would be hoisted with the apex up.

Des Davies, born 1926

Mr Fox

Every so often a tramp would come along the road and used to come and beg for food. My grandmother would give him a good meal, and a place to sleep up in the loft in the old warehouse that was behind the Mart. The old tramp, Mr Fox came from Manchester. He used to come every year so they wouldn't turn him away. They'd give him money or a bit of food to help him carry on. My grandfather was quite a religious man and he used to have a lot of talks with him and try and put him on the right way. He used to write every year to my grandfather and send Christmas cards. Eventually he found employment in Manchester and for years after, my father used to hear from Mr Fox

Gwladys Ednyfed Thomas

Albert Davies and his Human Seals

That was a con. Albert Davies was a good swimmer, used to swim Bala Lake and that sort of thing. In the summer there used to be a raft moored between the pier and the slipway, about a hundred yards out. Albert and his human seals would demonstrate swimming and diving for the visitors. The promenade would be lined with visitors. Albert was a good diver and he'd dive off the pier which is a fair old drop, you had to know what you were doing. He'd go down under the water and people would be saying, 'Oh where is he?' Jack Warrington, an old boy in his nineties, just like Popeye with his pipe, would be there sculling away pretending to look for him. Albert would be on the other side, hanging onto the lee side of the boat. Then he'd come up with a big splash. He didn't fool anybody really.

The payoff for the swimmers was that Albert took them to the fish and chip shop afterwards. I think Albert made quite a bit out of that on the quiet. He used to take up a collection. This was during the early and mid thirties.

Edward Ellis, born 1922

Albert Davies (in white coat) outside his shop in Great Darkgate Street, now the site of the Abbey National. The boy next to him is John Williams who later had his own fish shop in Chalybeate Street.

Dai Seren

Dai Seren lived about halfway down Cambrian Street. You could always tell when summer had arrived, when Dai Seren walked up the street in his white pumps.

Edward Ellis, born 1922

Major Stimson

Major Stimson was trained at Sheffield Physical Education College. He was loaned from the university to Ardwyn with Miss Arnold. She taught me lots of gymnastics when I was in the junior forms. Stimson was also connected with the Officers Training Corp. I was a good gymnast and had been out to Denmark on a holiday course and so forth. When I was at university I used to take a lot of his students.

John Lewis, born 1913

No Messing

Major Stimson was a great character and a fine figure of a man. He used to teach PE, was in charge of the local militia and the OTC. He had a place, Caerleon, on the prom and one day there was a rough sea and someone got into trouble. Old Stimmy swam straight out and straight back, no messing and rescued them.

Noel Butler, born 1913

Llew Williams

Llew Williams was a character on the prom. He had a long beard and big bushy hair. He had a boat, *Pride of the Midlands* doing trips to Aberdyfi. He'd be there shouting, 'This way to the motor boat, this way to the motor boat' on the prom, by the bandstand there.

Olwen Penney

Captain Rees

Captain Rees was my father. My father went to sea at a young age, from the age of thirteen as a donkey boy, making the tea and the like in the galley. He loved the sea. He had several ships, *Ambassador* and *Trident* were two of his last. He had one of the launches here, *Birmingham City*. There were seven altogether, doing trips in the bay and to Aberdyfi. From here to Aberdyfi and back was half a crown. He used to do a trip for nothing at night, back to the harbour for the children, crowds of children.

Birmingham City was specially built for him in Appledore in 1924. He just wanted something to do when he retired. Then the *Pride of the Midlands* and the *Worcester Castle* came, bigger boats. I often went on the boat but I didn't like the sea, neither did my two brothers. He died young, sixty-eight. He died in 1937.

Muriel Collison, born 1911

Daddo Jim

Daddo Jim, Silcock, used to live here in Trefechan. He used to hit us with his hat. Hard as iron it was with the salt. I think he had had it since he was a boy and it used to hurt. Norwegians the family were originally. He was a good sailor and had a boat called the *Snowdrop*. He was deaf as a post.

A postcard advertising Captain Rees and his motorboat Birmingham City, *c. 1925*

We had these trucks, a plank and four wheels. We were coming down High Street. There were two big wheels on the back with no rubber on them. I fell off see and of course I hurt my leg, right across. On the corner was Mr Edwards who had a Ford taxi. He took me up to hospital. They had a big pan of Iodine and I had to stick my leg in there and did it hurt! After I got home, Daddo Jim came in and wanted to know what was the matter. My parents told him and they wanted to know how I did it. Of course, being me I had to tell a lie didn't I? 'I cut it on some barbed wire down the harbour' I said. Old Daddo Jim goes down the harbour the next day and he looks for this barbed wire. He came over here 'There's no barbed wire down there, I've looked all over the place.' Of course I had to tell them the truth then. He took his hat off and gave me a clout.

Llew Bland, born 1917

Captain Brown

Captain Brown lived opposite us in High Street. He died when I was quite young. He'd been around the world many times. He was a very reserved gentleman. One street party he came out with all these gorgeous flags he'd collected on his journeys. Our eyes really popped out.

Pam Evans

Griffiths family

We used to go to Tanycae with the Griffiths. They were all good singers, good soprano voices. They did everything for the town because Mrs Wilkes, one of the daughters, was a very good organist. They were a family that did so much for the town and no one ever talks about them,

89

they seem to have been forgotten. Wilkes had a shoe shop opposite St Pauls. They used to run Tan-y-cae Sunday School and lived in South Road.

Phyllis Morgan

Ernie Carpanini

My side of the family were the Carpaninis. My father came to this country in 1911. He was only fourteen. He went to work in south Wales first. Mostly at that time they came from the town of Bardi, that's where my parents were from as they were poor there. They used to come to work for people who already had restaurants and cafes, so they could have a bit of money, work a year, go back and take some money home. That's the way they started. As they got older they were able to stay a little bit longer and put some money by for themselves. But the war broke out, the First World War, and a lot of them had to go back to serve with the allies. After they did their duty, they came back and carried on. They came back, brought their wives and started families. We came to Aberystwyth in 1929 but already Andrew Antoniazzi and his family were here. Mr Chiappa was my father's partner so it was Ernest and Joe years ago.

We had a cafe, the Mayflower Cafe. We called it the Continental to start with. It was in Terrace Road where the sweet shop was, the Bon-Bon. We had that for years then my father opened the fish and chip shop in Portland Road, Ernie's, and Mr Chiappa opened Joe's in Eastgate.

Leonora James

Some old Aberystwyth salts including Jim Silcock, third from left and Bob Humphreys, fourth from left.

They Never Let Us Go Hungry.

When I worked in the shop with my wife, we used to get people coming in. My father-in-law used to like to come down into the shop, not to work, but he liked to be there with us. More than once people would say, 'This man saved my life when we were in college here.' They were going back to the 1930s, coming here from south Wales, miners sons. They would say, 'We didn't have enough money to live but we could always come for chips and peas to Ernie or Joe and we could give them the money when we had it. They'd never let us go hungry.' I don't mean one or two, quite a few of them. They were marvellous men.

Roger James, born 1926

Happy Agnes

One character who every elderly person knew was 'Happy Agnes'. She lived in a garret over the arch leading to *Westminster Press*. 'Happy Agnes' was the original bag lady. People used to take pity on her and give her old clothes. If someone had an old dress that had perhaps gone out of fashion twenty years before, next thing you'd see 'Happy Agnes' going down the street in this dress. Another thing she was very fond of was hats. She must have had a great collection of hats, as lots of people gave her hats. Of course all the kids used to take the mickey out of her and she'd get quite annoyed. She used to carry an umbrella and I remember her hitting several people with this umbrella.

Des Davies, born 1926

Kate Pontin

Kate Pontin lived down somewhere near Skinner Street, that area. She used to wear a big tall black hat, long skirt and coat down to her ankles and carry a flat straw basket and walk like a man along the roads, not taking any notice of anybody. She must have been well in her forties when I knew her as a child.

Gwladys Ednyfed Thomas.

Harold Evans

Westminster Press was kept by Harold Evans, who was later secretary of the RNLI. He was a prisoner of war during the Second World War. If you've seen the film *Albert RN*, about the dummy, well he was in that camp though he wasn't one of the escapees. He was in the merchant navy before the war. The press went from there to Great Darkgate Street, at the back of Bradley, the clothes shop.

Des Davies, born 1926

Chicago Maud

Chicago Maud was Evan Jones' wife. She had skinny, skinny legs, used to wear a fur coat and had dyed blonde hair. She used to walk like an egg on legs.

Des Davies, born 1926

Evan James Davies

After the family's trawlers were sold, my father went to sea. He was on the *Mauretania*, the *Lusitania* in 1912 and the

Evan James Davies

was only a sergeant or something in the First World War. He really took charge. Everyone respected him and did what he said.

Glynne Pickford, born 1909

Yorkie

There used to be an old boy who used to come with rags and bones. He had a truck, Yorkie we used to call him. He'd be shouting and we'd chase after him.

Mavis Lowe, born 1924

Countess Barczynska

The Quarry theatre was behind the Queens, Rogues & Vagabonds run by Countess Barczynska. She was also an authoress, Oliver

Montrose. He was on the *Montrose* when Dr Crippen was caught. When war broke out he was called up as he was in the Royal Naval Reserve. He was on *HMS Jupiter.* There were thirteen of them from Aber and they got this medal from the Tsar. All this business came out after he died. My father told me they used to eat seal and the ship was all frozen up.

Des Davies, born 1926

E.J. Wakeling

Sergeant Wakeling we knew him as, used to boss all the processions in the area and get everything into order, the Mayor's Sunday processions and that sort of thing. I think he

E.J. Wakeling

Sands. Her husband was Caradoc Evans, the rebel author. Their son Nick used to walk around the town with a big sombrero hat. He was in film production, in London I think. Countess Barczynska, she was a character, really flamboyant. They lived near the town hall in one of those houses set back on the right. Harry Daniel was their chauffeur. He didn't like it as he'd be sitting up until two o'clock in the morning sitting outside wherever they were being entertained. The theatre wasn't bad, a bit rough.

Evan Andrew, born 1916

Andrew Antoniazzi

Andrew Antoniazzi had been in partnership in Abergavenny, I think with another Italian before the 1914-1918 war. The

Nick Sandys, son of Countess Barckzynska.

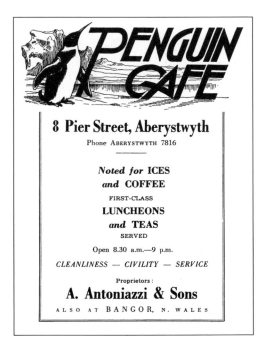

An advertisement for Penguin, c. 1965.

Italians had conscription and one of them had to go to war and it was Andrew who went. When he came back, his partner said there wasn't enough business for two of them, so his partner paid Andrew out and he came to Aberystwyth looking for a business. When he went to Pier Street he went in and saw this chap, he knew him actually, and said he was looking for a business. Mr Price said, 'What about this one?' The property at the time was owned by Mr Adler who was a hairdresser. Andrew paid for the business, well the stock really. When he came to check over the stock, most of them were dummies. Now my father was a wholesale confectioner and was going down Pier Street. He saw Antoniazzi in the shop in tears. Dad went in and asked what was the trouble. He explained what had happened and my father said, 'I will provide you with confectionery on a weekly basis and you can pay me as you can.' That's what set Antoniazzi up in business. Andrew bought the property from Adler the hairdresser further down [Pier Street] and developed it from there. I'm not sure when it changed to the Penguin, a good time after, because it was always known as Antoniazzi's. I remember as kids, we used to go in there for a fourpenny touch. This was really ice cream with a cordial on it.

John Lewis, born 1913

Fined Seven Shillings and Six Pence

Andrew Antoniazzi had the Penguin, and an offshoot which is now Morgans Cafe in Terrace Road. Every week in the *Cambrian News* you'd see that Andrew Antoniazzi was fined seven shillings and six pence for opening on a Sunday, week after week after week. In the days I'm talking about, a labourer's wage was only two pounds ten shillings. In that shop as a kid, I spent hours and hours there, sipping sarsaparilla. Andrew was on the committee of the football club and was very well liked.

Edward Ellis, born 1922

Ted Bevan

Ted was a really good, hard full-back. He came from south Wales. He was a big believer, if there was danger in the goalmouth, in kicking it out into touch. He

Aberystwyth Town FC 1937-1938. Glynne Pickford is on the extreme right of the back row, Ted Bevan is standing on the right of the goal keeper while second from the left in the front row is Gareth Hopkins who later signed for Stockport County.

94

was a very strong kicker, a very good footballer and captain for sometime. We relied on Ted very much to keep the back division keen. I was secretary, team manager and everything else for about eight years before the war and about eight years after the war when we were in the Cambrian Coast league.

Glynne Pickford, born 1909

Eddie Ellis

He was a good footballer. He could have chosen his club. He was like Michael Owen of Liverpool. He was a class above Aber.

Glynne Pickford, born 1909

Dick Arfon Jones

I remember my father telling me he left school at eleven, because his mother was crippled after his birth. He used to take milk around at an early age. He hardly had any education. He went to America, sailing as a kitchen boy on the ships that used to sail to America from Liverpool. He walked to Liverpool to pick up the boat, sleeping in sheds on the way. He remembered taking food in once when there was a fatal illness on the ship. No one would go in and feed these passengers because they had this illness. He was sent in without realising what was happening. He didn't suffer in any way.

My father was a fisherman but in the summer he used to take visitors out in the bay in his row-boat. Dad got this rowing boat and named it *Peggy*, after my mother. People used to come and stay in Aber for a week or a fortnight and used to get to know these fishermen. In the summer they'd be on the promenade and take people out to the boats, when the Navy were here, or take them out mackerel fishing. That's how they earned a living in those days. I remember taking my father's lunch and tea down to the promenade. They'd be there all day. On the top of the promenade they'd be touting then, taking a party of four or five out.

When the weather was rough they used to leave the boats on the prom in front of the Belle Vue. This was before the days of the *Worcester Castle*, *Pride of the Midlands*, *Mauretania* and all those. In the winter he'd be fishing, working on trawlers and that. He did all sorts of other jobs. He worked on building the sewage works, tarring the wooden pier, tarring the slipway, building the railway station, all sorts. Labouring on the station in 1927 he broke his leg. Fell off a ladder from the top. I remember him on crutches around the house and very upset because we had no money and my mother wanted me to go to school.

Dad then in the evenings was a commissionaire in the Coliseum when Evans had it before the Gales. They moved from Arbroath in Scotland. Peter, the son, was in my class in school. I used to go to the cinema nearly every night. His job was to get people in. He'd say, 'Come in, hurry up, only a few seats left,' but there might only be a dozen people in there. The Whittakers were the orchestra and Ned Lewis was on the drums.

My dad, he was in the Royal Naval Reserve. They were paid a retainer, which is why they all joined. Most of them were fishing for a living. He was called up to the RNR immediately. One of his ships was the *Jupiter*, I had a photo of it. It showed all of them lined up with all the snow and ice,

Pictured outside Teviotdales is Regimental Sergeant Major Fear with a number of Aberystwyth servicemen around 1916. Fifth from the left is Richard Arfon Jones, sixth from left is William David James, whilst on the extreme left of the front row is Evan James Davies. All three served on HMS Jupiter. Dick Jones is second from left in the front row. RSM Fear was instrumental in establishing the Aberystwyth Comforts for Fighters fund. This provided parcels containing chocolate, cigarettes etc for local servicemen during the First World War. These are probably the parcels in the photograph.

they were iced in. My father, he put on several stone because they were eating seals. He fell on the gangway with the slippery ice and damaged his back. The funny thing about it was, many years later as a commissionaire at the Coliseum, coming down the steps, he slipped and put his back right after many years. He came home from the forces, got married in 1917. I was born in 1919. My mother used to tell me she watched the Waterloo Hotel burning down and I was in the shawl. I was born in July. My mother came from Pontypridd. She came up with a friend, Hetty, when they were sixteen or seventeen to work in the Queens Hotel. My mother was a waitress in the Waterloo after the Queens.

During the war years for a short while he was a fireman. Again he joined the fire service as an auxiliary. After that he went into the fire service full time after he gave up being a commissionaire. When he finished as a fireman he stopped working.

He died at eighty-five, despite the hard life he had.

Merfyn Jones, born 1919.

CHAPTER 7

Streets and Shops

McIquhams China Shop, c. 1930. Now Rummers Wine Bar.

High Street

High Street is very different now, from when I grew up there. Everybody in the street knew everybody else. I think in High Street there were forty odd houses and everybody knew everybody in every house.

The shop that was on the corner opposite the Ship and Castle, was George Jones the grocer shop. When the coasters used to come to Aberystwyth that's where they used to buy their stores. He was a sort of Ships Chandler. He was there for years, then Rowlands took it over.

Des Davies, born 1926

Cacen Lloyd

At the side in Vulcan Street, there's an alley to the back of the Albion. Williams had a scrapyard there. At the back of this alley, off Vulcan street, was the back of Cacen Lloyd's cakeshop. Old Cacen Lloyd used to roast potatoes there and for a halfpenny you could have a roasty. The shop was opposite the market, where Gannets is. The door going into the shop used to be a stable door, in two halves. He used to have cakes in the window, with a mirror behind reflecting them to make them look attractive. The bread would be stacked up, and facing you when you went through the door was a shelf. On the shelf was a hambone, which he used to slice by hand, a big piece of beef and pork. Cacen Lloyd used to cook his own bread and cakes in the back. He was a bit of an inventor. He had a couple of certificates up in the back of the shop with his name on. My mother told me that one certificate was for the copyright for something he sold. On a tin of boot polish there's a little clip, well Cacen Lloyd invented that and that was what the certificate was for.

Des Davies, born 1926

St James Square

In that area by the market hall, opposite Reliance House, there used to be a

The corner of upper Great Darkgate Street and St James Square, later Beech's shop.

I. James, Grocer and Baker at the corner of South Road and Custom House Street, c. 1935.

newsagent and sweet shop which was Beech's. Mr and Mrs Beech and their sons, Sidney and John, used to live in number thirty-two High Street. He had these placard boards all around the shop. We used to get sweets for helping them take the boards in at night. Next door up, was Mrs Jones in the Swan. A lot of farmers used to go there because she used to cook a dinner. Just to the side of that was a very small shop. That was Ivor George's boot repair shop. He was a big fellow in the St Johns Ambulance. A bit further up, between him and Cacen Lloyd, used to be the Lorne Dairy. They used to make and sell their own ice cream. Tommy and Emrys used to play football for the town.

Des Davies, born 1926

Eleven Grocers

I can remember, that from South Road to Pier Street, there were eleven grocers' shops. Bitchell's Bridgend, also a post office, was where the butchers is now by Trefechan bridge. Birbecks was where Stoves'n'Stuff is now; Thomas was the house that Black Lion Fach took over; Williams was where the hairdresser is now, next to Gardiner's shop in Bridge Street. In Princess Street was Evan Jenkins, where I worked when I was twelve years of age. George Jones on the corner was also a grocer. Near the market was Mr Clark and his sister. Then there was Cacen Lloyd where Gannets is now; Morris where Richards the television was, that was a grocer shop-cum-dairy. On South Road

Thomas the grocer. The building is now incorporated into the Black Lion Fach.

there was James where Samy's television is and Thomas Tanycastell.

Evan Andrew, born 1916

Miss Phillips

Where Siop Enoc Huws is now, was a Miss Phillips. She sold sweets, yeast, Rinso washing powder and bundles of wood. Boy was she tight. If you bought a pennyworth of sweets and the scales went down too fast, she would break a sweet in half.

Evan Andrew, born 1916

Chip Shops.

Charlie Chips was the first in Bridge Street. When I was captain and we won the cup, there was a little fish shop by the town clock. Ernest and Joe had it then. Albert Davies give us all a dinner. We had a pennyworth of peas, a penny worth of chips and a bottle of Vimto. We thought that was great. I'd have been about thirteen. There was a chip shop in Eastgate, Sam Lewis had that. He was mayor after that. He was a boxer from south Wales. Ernest and Joe were in partnership together, then Joe took the one in Eastgate on. The town clock chip shop became a shoe shop after that.

Evan Andrew, born 1916

Cambrian Street

A lot of houses in Cambrian Street, including where I was brought up, specialised in keeping students in the winter and visitors in the summer. I'm talking about days when on five o'clock on a Saturday, the train would come in from the Birmingham area with people from Shrewsbury, Crewe and Lancashire. The train would have seventeen or eighteen coaches on it. You've seen the length of the platform! In the old days, trains that long used to come into Aberystwyth packed with families, coming for a fortnight very often. Cambrian Street was one of the places that had a lot of boarding houses of that kind.

There used to be a greengrocer down the bottom end, there's a cafe down there now. It was run by Leila Felix, that's what we called her; her name was Hughes, but Felix was her pre-married name. It was run by her for years. Halfway down Cambrian Street, where the gap comes where you look down Plascrug, you can see a large window there, that's where there was a sweetshop, run by Mr and Mrs Jarman, before they upped sticks and moved to Swindon. Later on it was kept by a Mr Nelson, then when he gave up, it ceased to be a shop and was transformed into the front room of a house. Also there was a little shop right on the corner of Thespian Street and Cambrian Street, a sort of butcher that specialised in faggots. You'd nip round there for faggots for your supper.

Edward Ellis, born 1922

Princess Street

There was a Shadrach Morris, where Ystwyth Books is today. They had two shops, one where the bookshop is, which sold really rough, coarse materials and suits for the farmers. The shop on the corner, which is now Benjamins, that was a more refined shop which sold materials and ladies clothing and so forth. But there was this character Morris, the old gentleman who used to sit in the shop in Princess Street, where the farmers used to go. It was mainly stuff for farmers they sold.

There's a house in Princess Street which was part of the Wesleyan chapel in Great Darkgate Street. The caretaker of the chapel, she was a Miss Lewis and she kept a small sweet shop. Then there was the New

Princess Street, c. 1930. Shadrach Morris' shop is on the left.

Misses Jones the milliners shop in Princess Street.

Quay Cafe where you could go and have a cup of tea for a penny. It had very ordinary food, sandwiches and what have you. I know my father used to have the firm Edmonsons deliver. They came from Liverpool I think, and they would deliver the confectionery to my father's warehouse and the two chaps who came, they would go into the New Quay Cafe and ask for water as they had tea in their canister. Miss Jenkins used to charge them a penny. Next to the New Quay Cafe was a milliner's shop, kept by the Misses Joneses. On the corner was George Jones, the grocer.

John Lewis, born 1913

Blue Gardens

I've always lived here in Blue Gardens. I remember who lived in all the houses. It's not like now, you don't know even whose living next door now. Next door was Mr and Mrs Blackwell. Mr Blackwell was a postman. In number four were two sisters who were the caretakers for years and years of Tabernacle chapel. In number five were the Davieses. Mr Davies was a wheelwright, mending wheels on the carts. In the house opposite, my godmother Miss Thomas lived. When you were small they were all aunties and uncles.

Florrie Bevan, born 1916

Bon-Bon

The Bon-Bon was run by a Mrs Longley. I remember her telling me she used to buy in two tons of Aberystwyth Rock. In those days it was a habit of buying a piece of rock to take back for the kids or whoever. Two tons a year she used to sell.

Eric Evans, born 1917

Upper Great Darkgate Street

Reliance House was a jewellers, Hugh Hughes. He was a mayor of Aberystwyth as well. Next door was the Angel Inn. Between that and the Farmers Arms was Gibby's Cattlefood. They had a small warehouse which later became my father's warehouse. Next door to the Farmers Arms was a Miss Morris, an elderly lady who was renowned for selling pickled herrings. She used to pickle them herself and also sold some confectionery, but the pickled herrings was the main trade she had. Next door to her was a dairy called Akers. Then Ernie and Joe started a fish and chip shop after the Akers moved out. Joe had been here a lot longer than Ernie and had worked for the Antoniazzis in Pier Street. There was a butchers on the corner where the fish and chip shop is now.

John Lewis, born 1913

Stalers

As kids we used to queue up outside Teviotdales or Wards, with a basket for stalers – yesterday's cakes that they sold off at a nominal price. These stalers we used to regard as real luxuries. We used to pay very little, say twopence for a basket. It would depend on how many were left. Cakes and the big cream buns were a real luxury.

Merfyn Jones, born 1919

Owen Hall's

There was a lovely delicatessen in Pier Street, same side as Galloways. The delicatessen was called Halls. They had foreign fruits and all sorts. The windows used to look so nice, very

tempting and the aroma of the coffee! Nothing was packed. When they used to weigh it, you could smell the aroma of everything. I can smell it now. It was lovely going into those shops, it was.

Madge Richards, born 1908

Sylvanus Edwards

There was a very nice grocery shop at the top of Great Darkgate Street, Sylvanus Edwards. He had high-class stuff. Nothing was packaged and they always looked so tidy. They would deliver things for you. They had lovely bacon and biscuits in jars, the best of everything. They weighed them then. You didn't have packaged things at all. They knew you as well.

Madge Richards, born 1908

Maria Doughton

Maria Doughton was on the corner of Bridge Street and Great Darkgate Street. Maria Doughtons sold little brass jugs, ornaments, little dolls, baskets, you name it she sold it. She was very sharp in the way she spoke to you. They used to say that she was hand in glove with the police. She used to tell the police all the little things that were going on.

Pam Evans

Star Supply Co

The Star was where Dorothy Perkins is now. It used to fascinate me, that when you had to pay, they put the money in those little containers, pulled the lever and it went whizzing to the cashier, then your change came whizzing back. I used to go shopping there with my grandmother and that really fascinated me.

Pam Evans

Williams Y Bont

There used to be a butcher, the other side of the bridge where the gardens are now, Williams Y Bont. There used to be a beautiful house there, Riversdale. It was beautiful, all oak beams and oak furniture, linen presses and a welsh dresser in the living room. You'd go there for sixpennyworth of something to fry or sixpennyworth of something to boil. You'd have a pile to come home with for sixpence.

Star Supply Co, now Dorothy Perkins, Great Darkgate Street, Aberystwyth.

On a weekend for five shillings we'd have a whole leg, not just the fillet off it.

Mavis Lowe, born 1924

Maypole

To see them in the Maypole with these huge mounds of butter and then patting them into pound and half pound blocks with the butters pats, that was fascinating. It wasn't pre-packed, neither was the tea nor the sugar. The sugar came in blue bags, between a cardboard and a paper.

Pam Evans

Terrace Road

I can remember the old arcade, Philips Arcade. That changed to Peacocks. On the corner, which I can't remember, was Fears, a fishmonger and poulterer. Boots took that over. The other corner, where the tourist office is, has been a number of things. Astons, the furniture had it and passed it on to someone else. Opposite there was the pub on the corner, the Blue Bell, which is an off-licence now. In between the Blue Bell and the White Horse on the other side, there was Joe Brennals, who came to the town during the war. It was a grocer's shop, J.C. Lloyd before. The corner, which is closed down now but used to belong to Ideal Bakeries and used to belong to Longleys before that who were tobacco importers. For all the tobaccos, pipes, cigars and all this you went to Longleys. Next door to that was the Continental Cafe kept by Mr Carpanini and Mr Chiappa. Before it was the Continental Café, it was the first

Rheidol Place, nicknamed the Bedlam, c. 1930.

Co-operative in Aberystwyth. They had two floors with a spiral staircase between the two floors. When it was taken over they made it into a cafe and residential upstairs. A different Longley had the Bon-Bon, the sweet shop. That's moved to where the cafe was. Between the Bon-Bon, and Oxfam as it is today, was a shoe shop, Morton's. W.H. Smith has been there as long as I can remember. There used to be a novelty shop where Acorn Fashions is run by a Mr Hodgkins, who was I think was from the Shifnal area. After he died his wife sold it as a going concern to a Mr Clark.

Further down was James Stores. You knew you were coming to James Stores because you could smell the coffee across the road. They used to grind it. You could smell all the spices that they used to sell loose. When you paid, the money was put in a container, they screwed the lid on, pulled the handle and sent it to the cash desk., like you see in old films. There wasn't one, there was about half a dozen. As kids we all used to go to see these things flying on wires. Then you had the pub, the, Glue-Pot next door. Next to that you had Roberts, the frozen meat where Dewhurst is now. Barclays Bank has always been there as long as I can remember.

Roger James, born 1926

Lloyds Tobacconist

It was fascinating, had wonderful smells. It was a real tobacconists it wasn't just a shop that sold cigarettes. It really sold everything, cigars, different types of tobacco, a great army of pipes and walking sticks, things like that. Roberts it was originally, but I recall it as A. Lloyd. He was a chap in his fifties. It was a genuine connoisseurs old tobacconists with lovely curved pipes and that sort of thing.

Edward Ellis, born 1922

Rheidol Place

I was born in Rheidol Place. There were eighteen cottages, we didn't have toilets or baths. If I remember rightly there were six toilets. The cottages were in three blocks, six in each block, three on either side. Eighteen altogether. We lived in number twelve.

My mother had a big zinc bath and used to bath me in there. My aunt used to live in South Road and sometimes I used to go there to my cousins and have a bath because they had more room. We had one room downstairs. Below, was a cellar which my mother did out and had a cooker in ultimately. She did most things on the fire, keeping a kettle going all the time for making tea. There was a tremendous community relationship which you don't experience today. Anybody walked into anybodys house. If anybody caught a big skate they'd hang it on a hook outside the house, then cook it and share it between those they were more friendly with. They always shared things.

Merfyn Jones, born 1919

Merfyn Jones, mayor of Aberystwyth in 1975 who grew up in Rheidol Place, photographed in his naval uniform during his national service.

CHAPTER 8

Public Houses

An early view of the Ship and Castle, High Street, c. 1910.

Pubs and Chapels

There were pubs and there were chapels and sometimes they overlapped. The notion that everyone either went to chapel or went to the pub is nonsense.

Edward Ellis, born 1919

Sixpence a Pint

You could get a pint of beer for sixpence. A pound note would buy you forty pints of beer. If you drank Robert's beer, which was five pence ha'penny, you could have another two and a half pints. Forty two and a half pints of beer for a pound. How does that make you laugh?

Reg White, born 1915

Old Mother Hubbards

It's still there, the Pier Hotel, but it was nothing like it is today. An old dear was there, Miss Wilkinson. It was nicknamed Mother Hubbards. This was just after the war. Coming from the beach, I was always in and out of the rowing boats with lobster pots. The old sailors and seamen, who were with the fishing boats doing two and a half hour trips in the bay, used to call there. They used to sell Banks from the wood. It was the best pint of Banks in Aberystwyth. Miss Wilkinson was the first woman I saw with a wig on. She used to take the beer out in a jug and fill the pints on the bar. She must have been well into her seventies. She had a low still where she put the hogshead. If the barrel went empty, half a dozen of the customers would have to go and put one up for her. There was a lot there who wouldn't go anywhere else.

Roger James, born 1926

Cracked Lino

The Pier Hotel was known as Old Mother Hubbards, it had cracked lino on the floor and all the seafarers used to go there.

Ted Salmon, born 1930

The Pier Hotel before its recent refurbishment.

John James Stores

John James, that's the pub. When you went in there and had a drink, that's when you were a man!

Evan Andrew, born 1916

Draught Bass

James's were the only ones in town selling Bass beer. I could never understand why they nicknamed it the Glue-Pot. There were various excuses, but the best was that once you were in there you were stuck there, you couldn't get out because of the beer. Inside it was primitive. As you went in through the door, they were all bat wing doors, the first door on your right was a lounge which nobody ever went into. Then you had sections partitioned into cubby-holes with benches and a table. The first time I went in there, I went through this door and there were about eight or nine, old girls, all at least seventy-five to eighty-five sitting on the benches, about five on each side and they had their half pints. That was their cubicle and nobody else could go in there. I was quickly chucked out. Next to that you had the long bar, the main bar of the pub. It was a continuous bar the entire length of the pub, something like fifty or sixty feet. Beyond that you had another five-a-side cubby hole and then you went around to what they called the back room. In the back room were the professional men of the town, people like Jessop the solicitor, Dalton the dental surgeon, that type. Old Davies the judge went, Hong Kong they called him as he was an old colonial judge. They would be in there from about quarter to six until quarter to seven, have a couple of pints, then they'd move out and go home for dinner. Then the ordinary rank and file would move in there. They'd be talking about various things, the town and so on.

The beer was drawn off the wood, there were no pumps or anything like that. There was no back entrance and no cellar, so to get the beer in there they had big stills behind the bar. They used to drop the wooden hogsheads down in Terrace Road, put a clamp on it with a chain and pulley and lift it up. That chain and pulley would slide on a rail right down the passageway and round the back of the bar until it came up on top of the still. They used to nurse the beer and I'll be quite honest with you,

James's Stores c. 1920. The door on the left led to the Glue-pot.

109

it was one of the best pints I've ever drunk. You couldn't get another one like it anywhere in Wales. The long bar was benches all around with a couple of wooden tables. The old boys that went there wouldn't go anywhere else. They never went in there for comfort. They went for the quality of the beer. That was the Glue-Pot, no finesse in there but the finest beer in Wales.

I remember one Christmas, you know how it is when the landlord give the customers a Christmas drink? In James's they sent up a hogsheads of Roberts' bitter. It was there for six months. The customers wouldn't take it for nothing. The customers going into James's I can remember them saying, 'No no, I'll have a Bass, I'll pay for it.' That only ever happened once to my knowledge.

Roger James, born 1936

The Fountain

The beer in the Fountain used to be from the wood. It was kept by a Mr and Mrs Lloyd. They were octogenarians. She could hardly see. You put a half a crown down on the bar for a drink and you'd be expecting two shillings back. She'd have thick lensed glasses on and she'd have to hold the coin three inches from her face to see what the coin was. Then the same procedure with the change to make sure she didn't give you half a crown back. It wasn't a busy pub by any means.

Roger James, born 1926

A Very Stately Man

Mr and Mrs Lloyd were there when I was a girl. They had a platform behind the bar

The Fountain, c. 1965.

South Road, c. 1930. The Sailors Arms is on the left.

because the bar used to be very high. Mr Lloyd was a very stately man with a white moustache.

Mavis Lowe, born 1924

Sailors Arms

The Sailors Arms was next to Tanycae. The last people to keep the Sailors Arms were the Lawsons. A lot of the lobster fishermen, who came up from Milford Haven when the lobster business was thriving just after the war, used to drink there. That was another pub with a lot of character. Like most of the pubs in those days, it was dark. There wasn't quite sawdust on the floors but it was that kind of place. It was very small.

Des Davies, born 1926

A Sailor's Pub

The two Miss Daniels kept the Sailors Arms when I was a boy. It was really a sailors' pub. I had a man who worked for me, Bill Lewis who lived in the bedlam. His mother died in her nineties. She was a barmaid there when she was a young girl and the men from the shipyards used to come and have their tots of rum, twopence a tot, before they started work in the mornings.

Evan Andrew, born 1916

Sailors Arms

Nana Daniel, Miss Daniel, an old maid used to keep it. Outside it looks much the same as it did then. As you walked down the steps you looked over the wall and there was a toilet. The pub was very small and dark and lit by oil lamps. I suppose we went in once or twice as kids to have a peep and see the old sailors drinking their beer and whatever else. You couldn't see them for smoke. Sailors Arms was a very popular old pub in those days. It was a bit rougher than the Castle.

Miss Daniel was thin and very proper and polite. There were chickens, down by the harbour where they built the sewage works, and she was something to do with them. Sometimes they'd get cut off by the tide and she'd have to paddle to go and fetch them.

Merfyn Jones, born 1919

Ship and Castle

The famous pub in High Street was the Ship and Castle. I was annoyed about it changing its name. When I lived in High Street, it was kept by the Roderick family. Later, in the 1930s by Tommy Edwards, who had been a ships' carpenter. After the war there was Will Lewis who been a policeman in London. It was one of the best pubs in town as it was a free house. Lots of characters used to drink there. I remember Daunty Simmonds drinking there. He used to live in Llanbadarn. He used to play the melodeon. He was always smartly dressed, a sort of gentleman's gentleman. The Ship and Castle was always chock-a-block. If the weather was hot then people would be outside drinking. It was a thriving business.

Des Davies, born 1926

Pubs in Trefechan

There was the Bridgend, the Black Horse, the Castle Hotel, before my time in where the pet shop is, the Three Tuns, the Fountain, one where the lodging house was, and one in Beehive Terrace. In my time there was the Bridgend, the Black Horse and the Fountain.

Watty Chamberlain, born 1906

Y Cwps (The Coopers)

I remember the Cwps when there was a snooker table upstairs. There used to be a league. They were playing in the league there one night and lost the black ball and were looking everywhere for that ball. Someone was drinking stout and the ball hit their teeth. How it got in there no one knows.

Ted Salmon, born 1930

A Jug

They had a decrepit old grandfather clock up in the snooker room in the Cwps. Instead of going downstairs to the toilet, they kept a jug in this clock for people to pee into.

Anon.

Merry Hell

A chap by the name of Bert was the landlord before Elfed. It was a very plain pub. It wasn't a bit like it is now. I remember working in the Cwps when Elfed was there, doing some plumbing. We were getting a water heater off the wall and some of the water went on the piano, his prize honky tonk. He played merry hell going on about this piano. Who was sitting in the corner, but a chap who used to be Prince Charles' bodyguard, a retired copper and he said 'You only paid two pounds fifty pence for it. It was on the way to the tip. What the hell are you shouting about?' Elfed said 'George Melly played on that piano.'

Ted Salmon, born 1930

Central Hotel

I met my husband when I was working in the bar of the Central Hotel. He came in for a drink and I met him there. It was very old fashioned, very rough in its way. There were spittoons round the bar and a billiard table for the local boys. You went through the swing door and passed the bar to get to the billiard table. It was on the ground floor. Captain Llewelin owned it. Then he died and I moved to Weymouth, but came back to the Central when Captain Llewellin's brother took it over. They had guests and a very nice dining room. It was very old fashioned, no running water.

The beer was kept in barrels in the cellar. They used to sell Robert's beer, brewed in Trefechan. Just mild, bitter and spirits. They were all on optics behind the bar.

Mild was sixpence a pint, sevenpence for bitter and eightpence for whisky. Old Dr Thomas used to nip in dinner time for his aperitif. He'd be the first customer in for lunchtime. Then a crowd used to gather with Captain Llewellin, the landlord, and they'd go through to a little room at the back, before you get to the staircase

Winifred Lavin

Black Horse

My grandmother lived next to the pub, only a little cottage it was. She had a passageway going down towards the yard and the side window of the pub used to look over her

The Central Hotel, c. 1950.

The Black Horse around 1930. Mrs Lowe's grandmother lived in the cottage next to the Black Horse.

garden. On a Sunday she'd have many a visitor coming into her house to go to the side window of the pub. They'd have a drink out the window. My grandmother was very popular on a Sunday.

Mavis Lowe, born 1924

The Unicorn, c. 1930.

CHAPTER 9

Trefechan

Trefechan c. 1930.

Turkey

Between the Black Bridge and Trefechan Bridge, was always known as Turkey and if you were born in Trefechan you were a Turk. As children we always used to fall out with the children in Tanycae and South Road. They daren't come down here to play. When we were having bonfires they'd come over on a night and try and light ours and we'd go from over here to try and light theirs.

Mavis Lowe, born 1924

Noted For Being Rough

Trefechan was noted for being rough. Turkey, Trefechan was called. We always used to fight Tanycae, South Road, with stone fights. They never came over the bridge, we always kept them the other side. Always stone fights and rough. The football team used to win the cup and were noted for roughness. Because of the lodging house and things, there were always two policemen coming down here.

Watty Chamberlain, born 1906

Zidon Stores

Where the shop, Zidon Stores is now, was a shop kept by Maggie Jane, a spinster. You used to go into a passageway and I remember the door to go in to the shop, the latch was a peg. She used to carry the peg with her and open the door. Every year the boys would win the cup and she'd put it in the window. We all had to go down to see the cup with ribbons on it, green and white. We used to go and watch them when we were kids. Trefechan were great.

Mavis Lowe, born 1924

Seven and Sixpence Rent a Week

There were two timberyards and a brewery. There was Meggitt and Jones where the flats are now, and Lloyd's timberyard where the fire station is now. Where Yr Odyn is, was just a mound, we used to play on there. My grandmother was seventy-two when she died in 1938. She was living in Glenhurst Cottages where Glenhurst Villas is now. She was in number one, next to the Black Horse and she was paying one shilling and tenpence a week, rent. When they built Yr Odyn she had the end one there. That was seven shillings and sixpence a week. She had an awful job to find the difference.

Mavis Lowe, born 1924

All My Life

I've lived in Trefechan all my life. I was born in Beehive Terrace, number two. When I was seven years of age we moved to the old pub that got closed, the Three Tuns, where Mari Parry lived. Later we came here and I've been here ever since.

The railway bridge for the Aberystwyth to Carmarthen Railway line.

Glanrafon Terrace, c.1920.

I can remember when I was very small, schooners coming in bringing timber to Lloyds and unloading it where the fire station is. The harbour wasn't as silted as it is now. They hadn't long finished working the lead mines. The *Grosvenor* would go from here to Liverpool and bring food and things in.

Watty Chamberlain, born 1906

The Green

I was born in Trefechan, in a house called the Green which has now been pulled down unfortunately. That and the adjoining house, the Lawn, were considered to be the best Georgian houses in Aberystwyth at that time. Bass, the brewery that eventually bought the old family brewery founded by my grandfather, they pulled it down and built this new thing and spoiled the appearance of Trefechan. It was just opposite the pet shop. It was a very good house, although it was on four levels.

There was a small hall on what was called the ground floor, but it wasn't the ground floor because that was even lower down where the kitchen was. Leading out of this hall was the staircase going upstairs. On each side were two good sized rooms. One was called the oak room because it had practically all oak furniture apart from the sofas and things, and the other was the dining room. That led, oddly enough, to the bathroom. The bathroom I suppose had been an addition at some stage. It was quite a nice sized room and it was over part of the ground floor where we had a wash house and that sort of thing. Upstairs from the small hall, there was the nursery on the left, a pantry in the middle and my father's room where he used to dress. The main bedroom was to the front of this. Eventually we had a bath put in there. On the other side of the nursery was a bedroom. Upstairs again there were the two maids' rooms, quite nice sized bedrooms where they could sit and look on to our front garden. Seems odd now, nobody has maids. At one time we had three. There were two girls normally and then the nurse came to look after my young brother.

Outside we had rather a nice garden. My mother was very keen on gardening and had a good wall built round most of it. There was a nice crazy paving going from the front door to the road and a lawn on both sides of it. On the one side of the house was the bottling department from the brewery. That was all pulled down when Bass took it over. I used to spend a lot of time tapping a tennis ball up against the wall and looking out onto Trefechan.

David Roberts, born 1912

The Lawn

The Wemyss family were great characters. They lived in the Lawn before the Wynnes. Colonel Wemyss came from southern Ireland and came with his family by ship. They used to keep monkeys and various other animals.

Wynne, the chemist who had a shop in Pier Street for many years, lived there after. He was one of the 'institutions' of Aberystwyth, I think a town councillor. The house had a big wing on the back of it and that went on fire on one occasion when we were there and caused a great deal of consternation. This wing was completely burnt out. The wing looked out onto rather a nice garden which formerly had been shared with the people who lived in the Green.

David Roberts, born 1912

For Charity

Mrs Wynne lived in the Lawn, she was related to Wynne the chemist in Pier Street. On a Friday night we used go there for threepence worth of flowers. Mrs Wynne

Trefechan as seen from Pen Dinas, c. 1937.

Old Cottages, Trefechan, c. 1930.

would come out, she was always very gracious, with a basket and scissors. We had to go just inside the hall, which was all polished and there was a box there and we put the threepence in the box. It was for charity. In the back she had a loganberry tree.

Mavis Lowe, born 1924

Brewery Stables

The stables had been especially made. My father was very keen on horses. We certainly had two, possibly more, they were Shires. They were really lovely creatures. They pulled the brewery carts all around the town and even as far as Pontrhydfendigaid. That was really a very great feat on their part as they had to go up a very steep hill beyond Crosswood. My father was always very anxious on the days they had to go up there

to know they had got back safely and would go and welcome them back, quite late at night sometimes.

David Roberts, born 1912

The Bragdy [brewhouse]

Across the road was the bragdy. It's a recording studio now. There they used to keep the wines and the liquor. I don't remember it being used to brew beer.

Mavis Lowe, born 1924

Gardening

There were two little houses overlooking the entrance to the road towards Tanybwlch, where we used to go for walks everyday, past where there is now a garage. Up in that area we had a very fine garden with vegetables and fruit. My mother was an extremely capable and keen gardener. We used to have the use of two men from the brewery to work it, dig it and all the rest of it. We had magnificent asparagus. My father used to send the horse and cart down to Tanybwlch once a year to get a good load or two of seaweed. This was then put onto the asparagus beds which apparently they like, so we had exceptionally good asparagus. We had raspberries, currants and things like that in a cage. Also pear trees, not much in the way of apples, lots of flowers – roses in particular, and rows of sweet peas in the summer. My mother used to cut basketfuls of flowers for the house. My father also took a considerable interest in the garden and arranged for a couple of chaps to be available to dig it and look after it. Now it's all built over.

David Roberts, born 1912

Radio Days

My father was very very clever with his hands and with radios. We had our first radio in 1923. The licence was ten shillings. My father used to make radios. He'd make the cabinets and the speakers. Many radios were sold from this house. He'd sell them for perhaps ten shillings or a pound. It was always handy because money was short.

The Black Horse and the newly built Glenhurst Villas.

The Sunday School or ysgol fach, *an offshoot of Tabernacle chapel, c. 1930.*

When we were in Spring Gardens, we used to open the front window and put the radio on the window and everybody would be dancing.

Mavis Lowe, born 1924

Sunday School

My father, Arthur Lewis, was the Sunday School teacher in Trefechan for years. They used to think the world of him because he used to tell them a lot of stories about the sea. He liked children. He could play the organ with no music at all. There were mischievous boys who would make a noise and disturb the service. My father would wait at the back and out he'd go, chase them, get hold of them and bring them into the Sunday School, walk them to the front 'There, we'll see your father later.'

Trefechan wasn't a good area but there were some very nice people there, very faithful, but it was pretty rough at the time.

Gwladys Ednyfed Thomas

Red Shed

The boys used to go down there gambling – the older boys. Us young 'uns were lookouts. Anybody that won would give you a penny. Even on a Sunday they used to go. My word, they had a summons to go to court for gambling on a Sunday! Nobody came down. What it was, PC Ishmael was on the other side of the harbour with his glasses, he couldn't actually see them, but presumed they were all gambling. They all got fined, five shillings, but they were never actually caught at it!

Llew Bland, born 1917

121

Traffic on the road through Trefechan, c. 1930.

Tip-Tap

We used to call after the policemen and pull their legs and call them names. They would chase after us. The police would always chase you for things. We used to put a piece of string across the street to hit their helmets off. We also used to tie two doorknobs next to each other then knock each door. Then you'd cut the string.

We use to put tip-tap on the windows. That was a bit of cotton hanging down from a drawing pin stuck in the window frame. You'd put something on the end of the cotton so it was hanging down and hitting the window. You couldn't see nothing from inside, but it was going tip-tap all the time. If they caught you they'd give you a clout, but they didn't do nothing else.

Watty Chamberlain, born 1906

Antagonizing the Police

There used to be two policemen at a time used to come down here, at one time. They was the old lodging house and the pubs here and of course there used to be rows. The boys used to tease the police like. One day there was a bit of a barney up at the shop. The police came down and told them to shift, that was to Long Stan and all the big boys. The police said, 'If you don't shift by the time we come back we'll book you.' 'You can't shift us cos we live here' they said back and there was a big row. The police went. Down the side by the harbour there were two boats so the boys took the plug out of one of them. The police then came back. The boys antagonized the police, ran into the one good boat, and went off. The police chased them and went in the other boat and it sunk. That was Alfie Lavin, Long Stan and those. There were some hard cases down here. One thing about it in them days though, the houses were never locked. You could always walk in, have a cup of tea and sit and talk for hours.

Llew Bland, born 1917

Pant-yr-Allt

Just before you come to the railway bridge you turn right and there is a road going up which takes you to the bottom of Pen Dinas. There was a row of cottages there. It was a doss-house, twopence a night or something. As children we were curious and our parents used to haul us along and tell us off for being so rude, for one thing.

You go up Pen Dinas, on the path that goes to the monument and there was a cottage on the left hand side there and a well where they used to get their water. The cottage has gone but the well is still there. I'll always remember going down that way for walks. It was lovely clear water.

Gwladys Ednyfed Thomas

The Lodging House

My husband, he was born in the lodging house. The lodging house kept going after the war, but there were only one or two there by then. My husband's father took the lodging house over from a Mr Owen, he bought it from him. Some stayed there for years. There were all sorts of people there, very quiet and no trouble. They only had a bed there and I'm sure half of them never

Pant-yr-Allt cottage on the slopes of Pen Dinas, c. 1935.

Pen Dinas showing the old isolation hospital, later the home of the Linnett family.

paid for that. They had to bring their own food. I remember old Mr Lavin, my husband's father, sitting there in the kitchen at night with a big fire in the corner. It was a big house. It's been pulled down now. There was a grass verge at the back where the water used to come up from the harbour.

Winifred Lavin, born 1908

Black Shed

They were gambling up here in the old Black Shed on the railway. Iorrie Jenkins, he broke his arm. The police chased them and they left the money and the cards. I think the police chased them along the line and Iorrie must have fallen down. I wasn't there, I was about fourteen, fifteen then.

Llew Bland, born 1917

The Storm of 1938

I remember the time the Linnetts were flooded out, it was the seven o'clock train that found them. All their stuff was out on the bank of the river and the cottage had gone. Our kitchen was full of water and we had to go upstairs. You couldn't get out through the back door it was that deep. It was a mess. I remember the Linnets and seeing the people going to rescue them. The Linnetts stayed in Aberystwyth, one worked for Dalton the dentist in Portland Street and the other was in the bank.

Winifred Lavin, born 1908

Keeping Pigs

My husband used to keep pigs and keep a nice market garden. He gave up keeping the

The Lodging house in Trefechan.

Alfie Lavin with his horse and cart in Mill Street.

pigs when he was sixty-five. He had over a hundred. Throughout he war he was exempt from service because of the lodging house and the pigs. He sold the pigs to Walsh and Baxters, down south Wales. He used to take them along the road to the station until the traffic got too bad. My husband had the last horse and cart in town. He used to go round all the hotels collecting the swill.

Winifred Lavin, born 1908

Mari Parry

We were living in the Three Tuns when she had the coach house and the stables. She was running trips on the prom and selling milk. She kept cows in the fields behind Dinas Terrace. The field on the side was where Mari kept her cattle. They've built houses there now. She used to buy furniture from Humphreys, the auctioneer. She used to go to the sales and then sell the furniture.

Watty Chamberlain, born 1906

A Tremendous Character

Mari Parry was a tremendous character, not vastly cared for by my family. She was always very dirty. She had a daughter called Sarah. Mari used to keep pigs and cows and had the land at the bottom of Pen Dinas where Dinas Terrace now is. She used to have a second hand furniture department which opened out onto the road which was quite interesting. She used to go to a lot of sales in the area and come back with quite good bits of antiques which she often used to sell for sixpence and which my parents used to snap up.

David Roberts, born 1912

Mari Parry's shop in Trefechan, once the Three Tuns public house.

A penn'orth of milk

When we were short of milk, we used to go to Mari Parry for a penn'orth of milk, and take a jug. She used to go to the cow and milk it while you were there. She had horses in the fields behind Dinas Terrace where they're building those houses, Felin y Mor. She had pigs as well.

Llew Bland, born 1917

Football

Longley gave out the first cup for the juniors, under seventeens. We won it, Trefechan Turks. We had a band, a lot of kids would go down with their big tins and would make drums – the Turkey Band. They all used to go in to watch us play football. It was threepence to go in. I played a bit for town one year when I was seventeen or eighteen and we won the North Wales Shield.

Watty Chamberlain, born 1906

Set Them Alight My Lucky Lads

Trefechan Football Club had their ground down on the 'aqua terra', now the camping ground. It was called aqua terra because it was under water all the time. My brother used to play for them when he was working for the brewery. Alfie Lavin was a great supporter and he used to shout, 'Set them alight my lucky lads'. They used the pub as a changing room. Mr Lloyd was very good to them.

Olwen Penney

Mr Watty Chamberlain.

Turkey Band

When we were kids we used to have a band for when the football team were playing, the senior team with Alfie Lavin, Tom Gerry and those. We used to have a band here with all the kids, loads of kids as everyone had big families in those days. We all had tins, Glyn Evans had this big tin, bigger than a television set and he was the drummer. We used to march all the way around the town, down the prom, along Terrace Road, up Great Darkgate Street, down to the football field. Halftime we used to go and sit in the centre circle and bang the drums and sing, 'Who said Trefechan couldn't play?' and all that.

127

Trefechan AFC 1936-1937. From left to right, back row: J.M. James (Treasurer), W.H. Lloyd (President). Standing: H. Feltham (Trainer), I. Jenkins, E. Morgan,, W. Isaac (Vice-Captain), B. Morgan, G. Christopher, Ll. Bland, D.E. Jones (Secretary). Sitting: D.E. Edwards (Chairman), A. C. Evans, I.L. Davies, Glyn Evans (Captain), J. Edwards, B.I Bradley, J. Lavin (Vice-Chairman).

We always had a song.

We are the turkey boys, we are the turkey boys,
We know our manners,
We spend our tanners,
And we are respected wherever we go.
And when we are marching down the great
     west road doors and windows open wide,
Then you'll here old Lavin shout
     'Put those bloody Woodbines Out'
We are the turkey boys.

This night they wouldn't let us in and Henry Roberts, from the brewery, came along. We told him they wouldn't let us in and he made them open the gates and he paid the penny or whatever for each of us to go in.

I won quite a few medals playing football.

Llew Bland, born 1917